The
Supreme
Wisdom

Volume Two

by
Mr. Elijah Muhammad
Messenger of Allah
to the Lost-Found Nation of Islam in North America

ISBN# 1-884855-92-X
EAN13# 978-1-884855-92-4

Published by
Secretarius MEMPS Publications
111 E Dunlap Ave, Ste 1-217
Phoenix, Arizona 85020-7802
Phone & Fax 602 466-7347
Email: secmemps@gmail.com
Web: www.memps.com

In the Name of Allah, the Beneficent, the Merciful

FOREWORD

You perhaps wonder why we call this little book "The Supreme Wisdom."
It is because most every word used in it is from the Lord of the worlds, "THE
SUPREME BEING," especially where you read of the History of the Caucasian Race; the History of the Black Nation and Prophets; the Doom of America—how she will be destroyed; the Hereafter; the Future of the so-called Negroes—"Tribe of Shabazz;" what happened 66 trillion years ago, 50,000 years
ago and 6,000 years ago. All of the answers are directly from the mouth of
Allah (God) in the Person of Master W. F. Muhammad, to Whom all praise
is due, the Great Mahdi or Messiah, as the Christians say, and He is also the
Son of Man.

He alone has taught me and continues to reveal His truth to me, although
to some it is unbelievable; but search your Scriptures and you will find that
they verify that which you read in this book—that which Allah (God) has revealed to me. If the so-called Negroes will accept it, they will be successful
and see the Hereafter. If not, they will be destroyed along with those who
are destroyed.

Say: He, Allah, is One God (not three), there is no God but He and I am
His Messenger and Servant.

— ELIJAH MUHAMMAD

Introduction

By Mr. Abdul Basit Naeem, Editor-Publisher, MOSLEM WORLD & THE
U. S. A. and THE AFRICAN-ASIAN WORLD, and Author
of "The Dead Are Rising . . ."

Much of the world of Islam today has succumbed to the onslaught of Westernism. The trend in Turkey, Iraq, Iran, Jordan, Pakistan and many other Muslim lands, in fact, is to continue to "do everything in the West's fashion," even if it means the total destruction of their National (Islamic) character and magnificent culture and civilization. So completely has the false but dazzling light of Materialism blinded the eyes of Muslims in the East!

A feeble little man in the U. S. A. —the mightiest of all Western countries —however, is asking those of his kind (the seventeen million so-called Negroes in America) to shed the West's "sinful and foolish" way of life—Christianity and all—and to rally around the banner of Islam (Freedom, Justice and Equality; Peace and Righteousness).

The man I am referring to, of course, is no other than the honorable Elijah Muhammad, author of this book.

The preaching of Islam among a peo-

ple whose belief in Jesus being God (which he was NOT) actually exceeds the limits of fanaticism, and whose churches and pastors have the powerful backing of the entire Christendom, is no easy task for any Muslim. The efforts of Mr. Elijah Muhammad, however, have produced much noteworthy result and borne abundant fruit, which proves that most surely Allah, our Almighty God, *is* with him.

I firmly believe the American so-called Negroes (who are not as yet the Believers) would do well to accept the advice of Mr. Elijah Muhammad, who is from among their own, and accept Islam as their Way of Life. It will bring about a great improvement in their financial, moral and spiritual condition and give them a status the like of which they have never known before. Christianity *cannot* and *will not* offer them anything better than what it has already given them. And, "Verily, Allah does not help a people except when they (show initiative and) endeavoi to help themselves."

Abdul Basit Naeem

Post Office Box 36
Brooklyn 21, N. Y.

Contents

Chapter Four:

THE CAUCASIAN (WHITE) RACE

Chapter Five:

CIVILIZATION

Chapter Six:

THE WORLDS — OLD AND NEW

Chapter Seven:

BABYLON AND AMERICA

Chapter Eight:

FEAR

Chapter Fourteen:

WOMEN AND CHILDREN

Chapter Fifteen:

THE BIBLE

Chapter Sixteen:

MY MISSION AND OBJECTIVE

Chapter Seventeen:

THE MUSLIM PRAYER

Chapter Eighteen:

THE HOLY QURAN

Chapter Nineteen:

WARNINGS AND PROPHECIES

Chapter Twenty:

WORDS OF ADVICE
TO MY PEOPLE

Chapter Twenty-One:
MISCELLANEOUS

Chapter Twenty-Two:
THE SUPREME WISDOM

Chapter One:

Allah, Our God

ALLAH, OUR GOD, IS ONE AND SELF-INDEPENDENT GOD

A Muslim is one who believes in One God (Allah).

It is forbidden by Allah for us to believe in or serve anyone other than Him as God.

It says in the Holy Quran, Chapter 112:1-4, *"Say, He, Allah, is One. Allah is He on whom all depend. He begets not, nor is He begotten, and none is like Him."*

Here Allah has clearly warned us not to set up an equal with Him, as He was ONE in the beginning from which everything had its beginning, and will be the One God from which everything will end.

Allah is also Self-Independent—having no need of anyone's help. And it's upon Him that *we all* depend.

It is the worst of ignorance for us to choose a God or attempt to make something as an equal to Allah. Foolish people all over the earth have been trying, for the past 6,000 years, to make an equal to Him, and are still at it—but how can anyone make an equal to such ONE (Allah) who had no beginning and for whom there is no end?

What fools we (the so-called Negroes) make of ourselves serving and worshipping gods other than the One God—Allah!

WE ARE DEPENDENT UPON ALLAH

Allah (God) is completely self-independent—having infinite knowledge and power over all—yet He is the most loving, the most merciful. But *we* are not self-independent; we are dependent upon Allah.

Only the foolish and disbelievers think and feel that they are self-independent and not dependent upon Allah.

ALLAH IS NOT A SPIRIT

The so-called Negroes think of God in terms of something without form (spirit or spook) and they believe that His throne is somewhere in the sky.

This is due to their ignorance of just what spirit means.

The teachings of Christianity have put God out of Man into nothing (spirit). Can you imagine God without form but yet interested in our affairs who are the human beings? What glory would an immaterial God get out of a material world?

We also learn that a spirit is not self-independent; it is dependent upon air, water and food. Without it, the spirit can have no life. So how can a spirit be God?

WHY WE MUST ACCEPT ALLAH NOW

Some people think that they should be left completely alone to believe in whatever they want to. They say let them be "free to serve God in their own way".

But we must accept Allah NOW, because we have been WARNED that one day all people will have to serve and worship Him (Allah) or be destroyed from among the people. And you and I live in that time.

God (Allah) would not be just to Himself and the law of justice to allow us to continue to do as we please about serving Allah and His true religion, Islam. I say that regardless of who they are who dislike Allah and Islam, they will be the loosers today, for the time has come that Righteousness must rule, to bring about Love, Peace and Universal Brotherhood.

WE MUST KNOW OURSELVES

Allah has declared that we (the so-called Negroes) cannot return to our own land and people until we have a thorough knowledge of our own selves.

We *must* first know ourselves!

THOSE WHO KNOW ALLAH LOVE, FEAR AND OBEY HIM

I know Allah and I am with Him.

You, the so-called Negroes who are not Muslim, also claim to know God (Allah), but you only lie in saying so—because those who know Allah love, fear and obey Him, but you love, fear and obey the devils—your open enemies—and not Allah, the God of Truth, Freedom and Justice.

ALLAH WILL MAKE HIMSELF KNOWN AND FELT IN AMERICA

America is the place where Allah will make Himself known and felt. This the whole world will soon know and believe.

ALLAH'S PROMISE TO ABRAHAM

The so-called Negroes will be taken away from the white Christians—it is binding upon Allah, to fulfill His promise to Abraham that He would return them to their own people.

WEAPONS AND THE BELIEF IN ALLAH (ONE GOD)

The Christians and Jews today, as they have done in the past, take the weapons of war for their gods and put their trust in them—the work of their own hands.

Muhammad (May the peace and blessings of Allah be upon him!) took hold of the *Belief in One God (Allah)* and he was successful. And fourteen hundred years later, *we*—that is, you and I who will not set up another God with Allah— are successful.

CHASTISEMENT FROM ALLAH

The so-called Negroes will accept Islam after they learn the truth of it and a chastisement from Allah, according to the prophecies of both the Bible and Holy Quran Sharrieff.

This is mentioned, for instance, in Ezekiel, the 37th Chapter, in which the so-called Negroes are referred to as "dry bones" who only needed the word of the Truth of Allah to be able to live again (that is, to become divinely civilized and independent of others).

The symbolic "dry bones" in the vision of Ezekiel, who had lost hope of ever being anything like independent—as other people—had at first refused to listen to the word of Truth and had to be whipped into submission by the winds (wars) blowing from all parts of the earth. (It is not the right understanding of the 37th Chapter of Ezekiel to say that it refers to Israel or any of the white race. The Holy Quran teaches that it is incumbent upon Allah to give life—the Truth—to the dead.)

ALLAH, NOT SWORD

The old Christian missionaries who wrote on the life and teachings of Muhammad, the Prophet, were his enemies. They were so grieved over the great success of Muhammad and Islam that they have written falsely against the man of God by attributing his success to the use of the sword instead of to Allah (God), from Whom it (Islam) actually came.

Muhammad and his followers were successful in their wars with their enemies because Allah, Whom they obeyed, was on their side. And Allah helped Muhammad and his followers because they fought for Truth and they were not the aggressors.

Here I might ask, is it the sword that is spreading Islam all over the world *today*, even here in America?

THE WORLD OF ALLAH

The world that the white man has built is nothing compared to that which Allah will build with his (the devil's) slaves (the so-called Negroes).

ALLAH IS PLEASED TO DEFEND US

My people: It is a pleasure for Allah to defend us from our enemies.

Allah is the author of Islam. In the religion of Christianity the white race had us and keeps us worshipping and praying to something that doesn't even exist. That's why Allah (God) alone can protect and defend us.

INSULT TO ALLAH

It is a perfect insult to Allah (God)—who made the heavens and earth, and Sun, Moon and Stars, and who makes the earth produce everything to serve our needs—for us to bow down and worship anyone other than Him.

The Great Mahdi, Allah in person, who is in our midst today, will put a stop once and forever to the serving and worshipping of gods besides Himself.

ALLAH IS ANGRY!

Allah has found His people (the so-called Negroes) and is angry with the slavemasters for the evil they have done to them.

He (Allah) will repay them (the devils) according to their doings.

ALLAH IS HERE, IN PERSON!

For the past 6,000 years, the prophets have been predicting the coming of God who would be Just and Righteous . . .This Righteous God would appear at the end of the world (of the white race).

Today, the God of Truth and Righteousness is making Himself manifest. He is not any more a mystery (unknown), but is KNOWN and can be SEEN and HEARD the earth over.

The teaching of God being a mystery has so enslaved the minds of my poor, ignorant people and they are so pitifully blind, deaf and dumb that it hurts; but I am going to prove to them that I am with Allah (God) and that He (Allah) is with me.

In spite of their (my people's) ignorance of Allah and myself whom He has

sent—for I am not self-sent—they and the world shall soon know who it is that has sent me.

God is here in Person, so stop looking to a dead Jesus for help and pray to HIM whom Jesus prophesied that would come after him. My people, pray to the One who is ALIVE and not a spook!

MASTER W. FARD MUHAMMAD

Before we ever suffered ourselves, Master W. Fard Muhammad, our God and Saviour, the Great Mahdi, Almighty God Allah in Person, Himself suffered persecution and rejection. All for you and for me!

THE GREAT MAHDI

In Rev. (18:1) it says that the Revelator saw an angel come from Heaven (from the Holy Land) having GREAT POWER and the earth (the so-called Negroes) was enlightened with His Glory (wisdom and knowledge of the Truth).

This angel can be no other than Master W. F. Muhammad, the Great Mahdi, who came from the Holy City of Mecca, Arabia, in 1930, and of whom we have spoken in many of our previous writings.

The Great Mahdi is indeed the most wise and powerful being on earth (God in Person). It is He who with a strong voice announced the immediate doom of America.

The Great Mahdi said to us that there was no punishment great enough to repay the slavemasters for their evils against the so-called Negroes of America. He also said that this country is filled with devils and every kind of evil.

His voice was strong and mighty, and to everyone who believed and accepted the True Religion (Islam) he gave a holy name of Allah's. Every word that he said is true. He came for the Salvation of the so-called Negroes, warning them to join on to their own kind (the Nation of Islam).

JEWS AND CHRISTIANS SET UP RIVALS TO ALLAH

Both the Jews and Christians are guilty of setting up rivals to Allah (God). Adam and Eve accepted the guidance of the serpent instead of Allah. (Gen. 3:6) They made and took a golden calf for their god and bowed down to it. (Ex. 32:4) This was the work of their own hands to guide them and fight their wars.

The Christians have made imaginary pictures and statues of wood, silver and gold. They bow down to Jesus, his mother and desciples, as though they can see and hear them.

The Christians also claim Sonship (for Jesus) to Allah (God), and take the Son to be the equal of the Father—though at the same time they say, "They Killed the Son."

THANKS, AND A PRAYER TO ALLAH

Thanks, THANKS to Allah, our God, in the person of Master Fard Muhammad, THE GREAT MAHDI, who was to come and has come, to restore we who were lost from our OWN—the Kingdom of Islam—and to destroy those who have destroyed us.

Thou art our God, O Allah, and we are Thy people. Deliver us from our murderers, and we will serve and obey Thee all the days of our life, and we will teach our children Thy Praises and to submit to Thee, for Thy unequaled Love and Mercy for us.

And thanks to You, O Allah, for making manifest our enemy (the devil), and help us, O Allah, to die the death of a Muslim.

THE BIBLE ON ALLAH (ONE GOD)

The Christians claim a belief in Noah, Abraham, Moses and Jesus—who believed in and taught of One God (Allah). But they also make Jesus the equal of Allah, despite such teaching of the Bible as follows, wherein God is said to have uttered these words: "I am the Lord thy God, thou shalt have no other gods before me. Thou shalt not make unto thee any graven images, or any likeness of anything that is in the heavens above, or that is in the water under the earth; thou shalt not bow down thyself to them, nor serve them, for I the Lord thy God am a jealous God."

13

Chapter Two:

The Original Man (The So-Called "Negro")

WHO IS THE ORIGINAL MAN ?

This question (Who is the Original Man?) is being answered from the mouth of Allah (God) to us (the so-called Negroes) for the first time since our straying away from our own nation.

This secret of God and the devil has been a mystery to the average one of mankind, and it has now been revealed in all its clearness to one who was so ignorant that he knew not even himself, born blind, deaf, and dumb in the wilderness of North America.

The truth about the devil is now being told and taught throughout the world, to his anger and deep sorrow. He is losing no time trying to hinder this truth of the above question, "Who is the Original Man?"

The devil, in fact, is setting watchers and listeners around me and my followers to see if he can find some other charge to put against us to satisfy his anger at the truth that we preach which is from the mouth of Allah, who is with us in Person.

The Original Man, Allah has declared, is none other than the black man.

He is the first and the last, and maker and owner of the universe; from him come all — brown, yellow, red and white. By using a special method of birth control law, the black man was able to produce the white race.

The true knowledge of the black and white mankind should be enough to awaken the so-called Negroes, put them on their feet and on the road to self-independence. Yet, they are so afraid of the slavemasters that they even love them to their destruction and wish that the bearer of Truth would not tell it (the Truth) even if he knows it.

The time has arrived when it must be told the world over who the Original Man is, for there are millions who do not know it. Why should this question be put before the world today? Because it is the TIME OF JUDGEMENT between the two (black and white) peoples, and to be without the knowledge of the Original Man means to be without the knowledge of the rightful owner of the earth.

HISTORY OF THE ORIGINAL MAN

Allah (to Whom praise is due) is

now pointing out to the nations of the earth their rightful places and this judgement will bring an end to *wars* over it.

Now it is so easy to recognize the Original Man, the real owner of the earth, by the history of the two (black and white) peoples. We have an unending past history of the black nation and a limited one of the white race.

We find that history teaches that the earth was populated by the black nation ever since it was created, but the history of the white race doesn't take us beyond 6,000 years.

Everywhere the white race has gone on our planet, they either found the Original Man or a sign that he had been there previously. Allah is proving to the world of black man that the white race actually doesn't own any part of our planet.

The Bible as well as the Holy Quran bear witness to the above fact, if you are able to understand it.

HISTORY OF THE TRIBE OF SHABAZZ

It is Allah's will and purpose that we shall know ourselves; therefore, He came Himself to teach us the knowledge of self. Who is better knowing of whom we are than God Himself? He has declared that we are descendants of the Asian black nation and of the tribe of Shabazz.

You might ask, who is this tribe of Shabazz? Originally, they were the tribe that came with the earth (or this part

of it) sixty-six trillion years ago when a great explosion on our planet divided it into two parts. One we call earth, the other moon.

We, the tribe of Shabazz, says Allah (God), were the first to discover the best part of our planet (earth) to live on, which is the rich Nile Valley of Egypt and the present seat of the Holy City, Mecca, Arabia.

THE SO-CALLED NEGROES ARE SACRED IN THE EYES OF ALLAH

America has poured wine into these sacred vessels of the Temple of God (the so-called Negroes). Let no man fool you concerning yourselves, my people. You are sacred in the eyes of Allah (God) today.

The so-called Negroes will have to be chastised into the knowledge of Allah, the God of their Salvation.

FEAR NO MORE, my people, for God is on your side today.

THE SO-CALLED NEGROES ARE GOOD BY NATURE

The so-called Negroes (descendants of the Tribe of Shabazz) are good people and very religiously inclined *by nature*. However, it is for the FIRST TIME that they are hearing of and accepting "the right religion in the right state," as it is stated in the Holy Quran. Islam, the religion of Allah, IS the religion of the so-called Negroes,

15

though their enemies may be averse.

My people, in fact, are inclined to righteous worship so much so that they are constantly seen disgracing themselves in their ignorant way, due to the lack of knowledge of their God (Allah) and His True Religion, Islam.

For the past 100 years since the slavemasters have opened the doors of their (Christian) church to them, they have gone insane over it. They have not taken a sane thought that if there were any saving power in the white race's churches of Christianity for them, why hasn't that POWER freed them from the slavemasters' children? Why are they begging them now for civil rights, which are supposedly given to any citizen by the Constitution? A slave or a free slave is not his master's equal. It is, therefore, silly for the so-called Negroes to think of being granted equal rights with their slavemasters' children.

Think of it!—They are a people who beg you to become a member of their Christian church and after accepting it with your whole heart, still you have to pray to them for recognition! They are ashamed to even call you a brother or sister in their religion and their very nature rebels against recognizing you!

"THE SACRED VESSELS"

If God destroyed ancient Babylon for the mockery made of the sacred vessels taken from the Temple in Jerusalem, what do you think Allah would do for America's mockery of the Sacred Vessels (the so-called Negroes) that SHE (America) took from their native land and people and filled with wine and whisky?

KINKY HAIR

The origin of our kinky hair came from one of our dissatisfied scientists, fifty thousand years ago, who wanted to make all of us tough and hard in order to endure the life of the jungles of East Asia (Africa) and to overcome the beasts there. But he failed to get the others to agree with him. He took his family and moved into the jungle to prove to us that we could live there and conquer the wild beasts and we have.

THE SO-CALLED NEGROES' PRESENT BELIEFS

It's a disgrace what the so-called Negroes believe today.

They believe, or are made to believe, that every religion other than Christianity is false and idol worship. In reality, it is the Christians who worship idol gods. Just take a look at the interior of their churches, or see their literature. They have statues of wood and metal and imaginary pictures of God, angels, prophets and their desciples. The Christians bow before these and revere the statues and pictures as if they could speak.

These statues and pictures, O my people, are NOT of God, His angels, prophets and desciples of Jesus. Those who worship them, therefore, worship nothing but falsehood and are ignorant enough to love it.

THE SO-CALLED NEGROES ARE GUILTY OF LOVING THE WHITE RACE

More than anyone else and those who worship his image, the so-called Negroes are guilty of loving the white race and all that that race goes for.

They (the so-called Negroes) hang the pictures of white people on the walls of their homes and one can find these (pictures) also on their mantle shelves, dressers and tables. Some even carry them (the white people's pictures) on their person.

They (the so-called Negroes) go to church and bow down to the statues under the names of Jesus and Mary and some under the name of Jesus's desciples, which, again, are only the images of the white race, their arch deceiver.

My people (the so-called Negroes) even worship the white man's names, which will not exist among the people of the NEW world, for they are not the names of God.

They (the so-called Negroes) would greatly benefit themselves if they would seek their places in that which Allah (God) is making NEW by giving back to the great deceiver (the devil) his religion (Christianity), churches and names, and accept the religion of their righteous Nation (Islam) and a name of their God (Allah).

98% OF THE SO-CALLED NEGROES DOUBT ISLAM

Ninety-eight per cent of the so-called Negroes are at the present time in doubt about Islam being their true religion. The other two per cent are with me— but they all will be with me as soon as they see and feel a little of the chastisement from Allah.

YOU SHALL NOT GRIEVE TODAY

Why should you doubt Islam when you know and have every proof that it is the Truth? Can you not put aside the fear that Christianity has put in your hearts?

Accept Islam, my people, and, by the Will of Allah, you'll be afraid no more, nor shall you grieve today.

WHY MY POOR PEOPLE ARE CONSTANTLY WATCHED

My poor people who have turned to their own God (Allah) and religion (Islam) are constantly being tracked down and watched—as though they were about to stickup a bank. This is done to try to put fear in them—so that they might stay away from their God (Allah), His true religion (Islam), and their Salvation and Defense.

"They (the devils) watch the steps of the righteous (the so-called Negroes), and seek to slay them." (Psalms 37:32) The so-called Negroes live under the very shadow of death in America. There is no justice for them in the courts of their slavemasters. Why, then, shouldn't America be chastised for her evils done to the so-called Negroes?

ONE DAY YOUR ENEMY WILL BOW DOWN TO YOU

You may not believe this today, but it will come to pass that even your enemy will one day bow down to you and show you the greatest respect.

Nothing but Islam will make you a dignified and respectable people, so join on to your own kind and accept Islam, the religion of Allah, which will put you on top of the world before you know it!

AFRICANS OF AMERICA AND SELF-RESPECT

The white people sometimes say, "If the Africans of America had self-respect and ability they would go to Ghana and help build a great African Nation.

But not with *their* (the devils') schooling!

If, however, the whites would stop interfering with those who are trying to qualify themselves for a return to their Native People and Country, within a few years they all would leave them (the devils) and their evil doings.

WE HAVE NO BIRTH RECORD

Allah has taught us that we the so-called Negroes are the original people of the earth who have no birth record.

THE SO-CALLED NEGROES MENTIONED IN THE NEW TESTAMENT

We the so-called Negroes are mentioned in the New Testament under several names and parables.

I will name two: the parable of the Lost Sheep and the Prodigal Son (Luke 15:1-11), of which we could not be described better under or in a parable.

Before the coming of Allah (God) we, being blind, deaf and dumb, had mistaken the true meanings of these parables to be referring to the Jews. Now, thanks to Almighty Allah, who came in the Person of Master Fard Muhammad (to whom be praised forever), who has opened my blinded eyes, loosened the knot in my tongue, and has made us to understand that these Bible parables are referring to us, the so-called Negroes (and our slavemasters).

The answer (Luke 15:4-6) to the charges made by the proud and unholy Pharisees against Him (God in Person) for eating with His lost-found people whom the Pharisees and their people had made sinners can't be better. It defends Him and His people (lost and found sheep). He proved their wickedness and hatred for His love for His people who were lost and He had found them. They (the Pharisees) had more love for a lost and found animal of theirs than they did for the lost and found people of Allah (God).

Chapter Three:

Jesus, Christianity and Christians

CHRISTIANITY IS NOT FOR BLACK PEOPLE

The archleader of "Christian Party" in Atlanta, Georgia, had told the truth in his letter printed recently in a newspaper and MOSLEM WORLD & THE U. S. A. magazine when he said that "Christianity has been successful in white nations among the white people, but does not appear to have roots in any colored (black) nation."

I thank him for bearing witness with me that the false white Christian religion was for his (white) race, and not for the black people. The black nation's religion is Islam and its God is Allah, the author of Islam, and not the Pope of Rome.

No black people can be successful trying to play the white race's game of civilization; they will only be trapped by them as their slaves.

CHRISTIANITY IS NOT FROM ALLAH

A religion used by the devils to convert people, especially when it didn't come from Him, cannot be accepted by Allah.

We know that Christianity came from the white race, and it is not from Allah.

CHRISTIANITY IS ONLY FOR THE WHITE RACE

Many white people know and believe that Christianity is only for the white race, and that the so-called Negroes' religion is Islam. But they (the devils) won't teach it (Islam) to their poor black slaves or even leave them alone in their search for knowledge of Allah and His Divine Religion.

CHRISTIANITY BELONGS TO WHITE EUROPE AND AMERICA

Black Africa should have learned her lesson from Christianity long ago and driven it back to white Europe and America where it belongs.

CHRISTIANS' "ONE GOD"

The Christian believers claim that they believe in "One God."

Yet they worship gods other than Allah, the Divine Supreme Being, and make His Angels and Prophets His (God's) equals.

Should not Allah destroy those who serve and worship gods other than He?

JEWS AND CHRISTIANS ARE NOT ALLAH'S "BELOVED ONES"

"And the Jews and Christians say: 'We are sons of Allah and His beloved ones.' Say: 'Why does He then chastise you for your faults?"—THE HOLY QURAN 5:18.

The Christian whites claim nearness to Allah (God) and make Jesus a member of their wicked race and ascribe Sonship unto him. The Jews also claim to be God's "beloved ones."

These sayings of theirs have deceived the so-called Negroes in America one hundred per cent, and many black people throughout the earth.

The Jews and Christians are NOT really the "beloved ones" of Allah.

Because of the prosperity they have enjoyed in this world, they think that they are the beloved people of Allah. They don't know, but soon they will, that they were deliberately given a great time of prosperity and that it is to be followed with destruction.

Besides, if they are the beloved of Allah, why aren't they good people? And why don't they live the life of prophets they claim to be following.

The Jews and Christians have been successful in deceiving the whole world of dark mankind, as to the truth about themselves by killing the prophets of Allah. They even seek to take *my life* today because I teach the truth of Allah which gives life to my people whom they have killed mentally.

CHRISTIANITY TEACHES YOU TO LOVE YOUR ENEMIES

Christianity is a religion that teaches you to love your enemies and hate your friends, and to seek reward after death. It has produced more division and hate than all the other religions combined.

WHERE IS CHRISTIANS' LOVE?

The Christians say that Jesus taught them love. Where is this love of theirs?

Allah says of them: *"We excited among them enmity and hatred to the day of resurrection; and Allah will inform them of what they did."—THE HOLY QURAN 5:14.*

This is a manifest truth. The white race is not at peace with each other. Can we seek peace among such evil, hateful and bloodthirsty people? They hate you and I (the so-called Negroes) so much that they dislike seeing us live in peace in their midst.

CHRISTIANITY PERMITS EVIL PRACTICES

The Christian religion permits every evil practice that is known to mankind. It's a shame that such religion and people they (the Christians) call to be of Jesus!

JESUS CANNOT HEAR YOU PRAY

Know that Jesus was only a prophet and cannot hear you pray any more than Moses or any other dead prophet. Allah alone can hear your prayers and answer them.

"HOW CAN A DEAD MAN HEAR AND SAVE PEOPLE?"

The white Christians preach that Jesus, whom they killed 2,000 years ago, will hear and save the so-called Negroes. Let them prove that lie! How can a dead man hear and save people?

You are not taught to pray to be heard by Moses and other prophets, not even Elijah, who, they say, went to Heaven whole soul and body. If Elijah cannot hear a prayer, and he was not killed as Jesus was, then how can Jesus hear a prayer?

We must not pray to dead prophets. They cannot hear our prayers.

DRINKING, JESUS AND MY PEOPLE

Many white people accuse the so-called Negroes, who are really members of the Holy Tribe of Shabazz, of being drunkards and thieves, and (wrongly) advise them to oppose Islam because it forbids Muslims to drink intoxicating drinks.

I would like to ask the accusers: Who makes the intoxicating drinks—the white Christians or the so-called Negroes? And doesn't their (Christian) government legalize the sale and drinking of strong drinks? And did they (the devils) find that my people were thieves and drunkards in their Native Land, four hundred years ago, when they were kidnapped by John Hawkins and brought over here into slavery? And haven't the white people been their master and teacher since? Then whatever my people (the so-called Negroes) are today, the devils (the white Christian race) made them that.

SWORD AND CHRISTIANITY

According to the Bible (Matthew 10: 34), Jesus didn't come for peace but to bring the sword. Neither did he come to unite. (Matthew 10:35) It stands true today that Christianity, as we see it in practice in America, certainly does not unite but rather divides the people against each other. According to the history of it, Christianity has caused more bloodshed than any other combination of religions; its sword is never sheathed.

If Jesus was a peacemaker, then the Christians are not his follwers.

THE SIGN OF CHRISTIANITY

The Cross (the sign or emblem) of Christianity represents the physical workings of that religion. The Cross is far from being a sign of a true religion. If a religion's base (foundation) or sign is not found in the universal order of things, it cannot be called the religion of Allah (God), nor can it be called a "religion in the right state."

My people, the so-called Negroes, should never wear a cross as a sign for his or her salvation, for it is just the opposite.

CHRISTIANS – THE FIRST-RATE HYPOCRITES

The Bible teaches (the Christians) against the doing of evil. It also warns them to "do unto others as you would have done unto yourselves" and to "love thy brother as thyself."

Not any of these teachings have the white Christians or their kind ever practiced

They (the white Christians) do not care for a so-called Negro Christian believer to call him their brother Christian. And they do not think of doing unto him (the so-called Negro Christian believer) as they would have done unto themselves. The devils beat and kill them (the so-called Negroes) day and night and bomb their churches, where in reality they worship the white race, not Jesus. They even burn their own Christian sign (the Cross) when they plan to kill or burn their poor black Christian slaves.

They (the white Christians) are, therefore, hypocrites of the first order.

CHRIST-HATING

Some people allege the Muslims to be "Christ-hating." Let me tell them that in making such baseless allegations they use the name of Jesus only for a bait to deceive the so-called Negroes, while at the same time they are not doers of the teachings of Christ, nor of the Prophets before Jesus.

JESUS OF THE BIBLE

The so-called Negroes must get away from the old slavery teaching that Jesus, who died two thousand years ago, is still alive somewhere, waiting for and listening to their prayers.

He (Jesus) was only a prophet like Moses and the other prophets and had the same religion (Islam). He did his work and is dead like others of his time, and has no knowledge of their prayers to him.

Since Islam over-ran the world in the 7th Century after Jesus and is still a power of man, why didn't the translators of the Bible mention it? Why didn't they give us the names of the religions of the prophets since they claim a religion for Jesus?

The history of this man Jesus has been greatly misunderstood by us, the so-called Negroes.

Chapter Four:

The Caucasian (White) Race

THE CAUCASIAN RACE

Out of nothing it was that the present universe was created, and out of the weak of the BLACK NATION the present Caucasian race was created.

I would like the Christians among my people, who say they are believers in the Bible and Jesus, to read and study the Chapter of John 8:42-44. It says in there, "If God was your Father, you would love me." If you understand it right, you will agree with me that the whole Caucasian race is a race of devils. They proved to be devils in the Garden of Paradise and 4,000 years later they were condemned by Jesus. Likewise, they are condemned today by the Great Mahdi Muhammad as being nothing but devils in the plainest language.

Surely, if the Father of the two people (black and white) was the same, the two would love each other. In a family where the children are of one father they love each other because they are of the same flesh and blood.

It is natural then for them to love each other. Again, it is not unnatural then for a member or members of a different race or nation not to love the non-member of their race or nation as their own.

The argument here (between Jesus and the Jews) is that the Jews claimed they were the same people, children of one God (or Father), but this Jesus disagreed with and proved they were not from the same Father (God). He (Jesus), having a knowledge of both Fathers, knew their Father (Devil) before his fall and before he had produced his children (the white race) of whom the Jews are members. Here, in this Chapter (John 8), it shows there was no love in the Jews for Jesus.

THE CAUCASIAN RACE'S WORLD

The world that the Caucasian race built (the present world) is full of evil and bloodshed and one in which there is no peace for the black nation—the real owners of the earth.

But that which was to be, must be; and, likewise, what *is to be, will* be. So, the present world of sin will come to an end, to be replaced by a New World of righteousness.

WHITES NO LONGER RULE BLACK ASIA

The whites (Christians) have lost the power of attraction and rule over black Asia, and, in their frenzied effort to restore it, are now running all over the world trying to deceive the black nation, so as to allow them time to continue their wicked rule of injustice.

WHY DON'T THE WHITE PEOPLE LEAVE US ALONE?

Many white Christians boast of America being a white man's country, but why did they bring US here? And if the white race is such a superior race, why don't they live alone—and leave US to live alone in *our* own country? Why are they fighting to stay in Asia? Why aren't they satisfied with Europe and America?

The white people should know that we did not *ask* them to bring us here.

WHITE MAN'S CHRISTIANITY

White man's Christianity has robbed us of the knowledge of self and kind and destroyed our peace and love for one another

WE CAN LIVE WITHOUT WHITE PEOPLE

Some people say that we can't live without the white race to rule us. I am sorry for the so-called Negroes who would believe anything so false.

We CAN and WILL live without the white race to rule us, as we did for millions of years before the devil's appearance on our planet.

THE WHITE PEOPLE ARE NOW BEING REVEALED

The TIME given the white people by Allah to rule the world (6,000 years) is now up and they are being REVEALED. This means the whites will by no means be able to hide themselves (their true nature) or deceive my people (the so-called Negroes) any longer.

THE WHITES WILL NEVER TURN MUSLIM

Some Arab Muslims think that the white people can be made Muslims but NOT ME! The devils and their kind will not accept Allah and His religion of Righteousness (Islam) unless they are really born again. And it is too late for a rebirth!

THE MIXING OF BLACK AND WHITE BLOOD

I want to make this very clear that my people (the so-called Negroes) have not been and are not today interested in the mixing of their blood with the whites' blood.

The black Africans *never* went seeking white women in Europe, and if there are any white women in Africa today the devil himself took them there. And isn't it true that black Africans everywhere (in Africa) today are demanding that the white man leave their people and country—to prevent, among other things, the further mixing of their blood with whites'?

And as for the so-called Negroes of America, they cannot be blamed for any mixing of the blood here, because, in the first place, they did not come to this Western world of their own desire and were brought from their Native Land and People *against their will*. Besides, did the so-called Negro slaves ever try to make love with their slavemasters' wives and daughters, while they (the devils) held (as they still hold) complete power over them? And which of the houses and families show that the black or white males have been and are still visiting— yours or the so-called Negroes?

My people (the so-called Negroes) see the white people of both sexes day and night after black men and women— whistling, winking their eyes, and blowing their car horns at them, and making love to every so-called Negro woman that walks, rides, flies, or works for the devils in their homes, offices and factories.

Not in America alone but all over the earth wherever you go among the black, brown, yellow, and red people, we see the white people after our women, whom they say to be "ugly." (If the so-called Negro women are "ugly," why then do they attract the whites and their kind?) The devils, in fact, and according to history, have been after our women ever since being on our Planet.

The white race was driven out of Asia six thousand years ago, to keep them away from black women and to prevent them from mixing their wicked blood with that of the Native People. We veiled and even locked our black women in, to keep the devils' blue eyes from feasting on

their beauty. And the only solution to this mixture of the devils' blood in our homes today is that Allah remove them completely off our Planet, also those who desire mixing with them. This is the *Resurrection* and separation of us all; little do the whites and the so-called Negroes know or believe it!

THE KNOWLEDGE OF WHITE RACE REMOVES ALL MISUNDERSTAND-ING

A true knowledge of the white race removes once and for all times the mistakes that would be made in deal- ing with them. My followers and I can and are getting along with them in a more understandable way than ever, because we know them.

You can't blame one for the way he or she was born, for they had nothing to do with that. Can we say to them why don't you do righteousness when Nature did not give righteousness to them? Or can we say to them why are you such a wicked devil? Who is re- sponsible—the made or the maker? (The white man did not make him- self.)

Yet this does not excuse us for fol- lowing and practicing his evil habits or ac- cepting him for a righteous guide just because he is not his maker.

WHITE RACE'S DAY IS OVER

I must keep warning you that you

should give up the white race's names and religion in order to gain success. Their days of success are over; their rule will last only as long as you remain asleep to the knowledge of self.

Awake and know that Allah has RE-VEALED the Truth. Stop believing in something coming to you after you are physically dead. That is untrue and no one can show you any proof of such belief.

WORDS OF ADVICE TO WHITE PEOPLE

No white people ever tell us who brought them and their race into civilization when they were walking on "all-fours", climbing trees, living in hills and caves of Europe, just 4,000 years ago! Was it one of their own "super" whites or one of our blacks? Who put them there—they did it themselves or did we put them there? Where did their race first see the black man—in the jungles of Africa or across the border east of Europe, living in beautiful cities and homes? Who did they find in the Western Hemisphere when they "discovered" it—their people or our people? Who created the heavens and the earth—our Father or theirs? Who created their race itself—they or one of our Nation? Can they claim this earth or any other planet to be that which their fathers created?

The white people should also know who has started the dust storms and earthquakes in their country—their kind or Allah?

Some white people go as far as threat-ening to expel us from America. Drive us out and see how long you will remain! (But if we drive you out, we will live forever without you, as we did before you.)

My advice to the white race is that it better keep silent as to who shall live on this planet, for they haven't anything that is theirs. This is OUR earth!

Be happy, white folks, that you have the so-called Negroes in your midst, and especially those who are Muslims, for if they were not (in your midst) you wouldn't last very long!

THE WHITE CHRISTIANS

It was white Christians who brought our forefathers into slavery, and it is their false religion that is keeping you a subject people today. They rape and murder your families and bomb your homes and Churches if you demand equal rights with them and justice. The white Christians don't want you, nor do they like to see you go from them to your own. They fear your unity with your own.

ONLY THE IGNORANT SO-CALLED NEGROES LOVE WHITES

The only so-called Negroes who love the white people and desire them for friends are those who are ignorant of the knowledge of their race and kind. And as soon as they awaken to it—to the knowledge of the devils' race and kind— they too will not want to love them, or even shake their hands or look at them (or their shadow!).

THE TRUTH OF WHITE RACE WILL MAKE ALL BLACK MANKIND HATE THEM

The Truth of the white race and kind will make all black mankind hate them, regardless of their color—black, brown, yellow or red.

This TRUTH of the white race is part of that secret that was withheld by Allah to allow them (the devils) to live their TIME (6,000 years).

MAN OF SIN

The man of sin referred to in the Bible (II Thessalonians 2:3) is now being revealed. He is the devil in person who was made of sin, not any good was in the essence that he was from. Since he was made of sin, what good can one expect of the man of sin?

Why has he (the man of sin) been hidden from the eyes of the righteous people and only revealed today? The answer is: How could the man of sin rule the righteous for six thousand years if he had not been veiled to prevent the discovery of his true self?

According to II Thessalonians 2:9, the man of sin had work to do and God wouldn't interfere with this work of the man of sin until the time given him was fully up.

The eighth verse in II Thessalonians reads that the Lord shall consume with the Spirit (of Truth of the man of sin) of his mouth, and shall destroy with the Brightness of His Coming, which means that the truth of the man of sin is clearly

made by God that there can be no doubt that he is really the man of sin who has caused and is causing all the trouble among the righteous. He (the man of sin) is a great deceiver, liar and a murderer by nature.

THE DEVIL'S LIES

The whites of this country make the so-called Negroes do for them everything that a real citizen does, and yet they will not give them equal rights as a citizen. They make my people (the so-called Negroes fight to keep them (the devils) free to rule them and their kind

The so-called Negroes pay equal taxes but are paid the lowest wages. In certain states, such as Georgia, they aren't allowed to use the (white-operated) highway filling stations' rest rooms (but will be arrested if seen relieving themselves in public). They are not allowed to eat in public eating places, though they may purchase the food and eat it on the outside. Yet when America's future is at stake, the devils tell my people that it is *their* country and that they *are* citizens of it.

My people should know that they are fools for believing what the slavemasters (their open enemies) say, knowing that they have told them the same old false story many times.

If there was any good in the white people (which there isn't) they would exempt all the so-called Negroes—their free slaves—from paying taxes, especially when the devils don't intend to divide their forty-eight states with them, not even one state, nor the spoils of war that they so willingly help gain for them.

Chapter Five:

Civilization

TYPES OF CIVILIZATION

There are several civilizations; we have a wicked one and a righteous one. It is a righteous civilization that is in the workings now. We all have been well-trained into the wicked civilization; now we must be trained into the knowledge of the righteous one. We MUST have a righteous-trained, civilized man, who will not fail to perform his duty to us in guiding and teaching us.

SPIRITUAL CIVILIZATION

The duty of a civilized man is to teach civilization and the arts and sciences of civilized people to the uncivilized.

The duty of a Divine Messenger, raised by Allah Himself, is to teach his people spiritual civilization, which is important and necessary for the success of a society. According to history, the people who refuse to accept Divine Guidance or Allah's Message brought by His Messengers are classified as uncivilized or savages.

A well-educated, cultured and courteous people make a beautiful society when it is spiritual. Good manners come from the civilized man who doesn't fail to perform his duty.

THE RIGHTEOUS CIVILIZATION

My people in America, the so-called Negroes, are under the searchlight of the righteous, who are offering to them the right guidance to supreme civilization of righteousness, never witnessed before on earth. The white race has failed to perform its duty of civilizing the American so-called Negroes. Of course, they have been their slaves for many centuries, and the slavemasters have rights over them, as long as they are (the slavemasters') slave. However, if the slavemasters free their slaves—not in words but in deeds—the slavemasters should provide the once-slaves with the right civilization and with everything necessary for them to start an INDEPENDENT life as their slavemasters have.

Certainly, the so-called Negroes are being schooled, but is it the equal of their slavemasters? No, the so-called Negroes are still begging for the equal education. After being blinded to the knowledge of self and their own kind for 400 years, the slavemasters refuse to civilize the so-called Negroes into the knowledge of ·themselves of which they were robbed. The slavemasters also persecute and hinder anyone who tries to perform this most rightful duty.

I will continue to say that as long as the so-called Negroes don't know who they really are and do not have the knowledge to free themselves from their slavemasters' names and religion, they can't be considered civilized.

Chapter Six:

The Worlds — Old and New

LIFE OF THIS WORLD: SPORT AND PLAY

The life of this world, as the Holy Quran tells us, is nothing else but sport and play. Such world has and is attracting the members of the Righteous (Nation of Islam) to take part in it. Good is not wanted by this wicked world.

Turn to Allah, my people, for there is no God but Him, and He will turn to you and protect you from the evils of this world.

THE PRESENT WORLD IS AGAINST THE TRUTH

"And the dragon (the devil) stood before the woman, who is pregnant (the messenger of Allah, bearer of the life-giving Truth), to devour her child (to hinder the truth from being believed by the people of the messenger) as soon as it was born." (Rev. 12:4)

The present world (of the devils) is thus against the Truth and is doing everything in its power to prevent it (the Truth) from reaching the hearts of my people (the so-called Negroes).

CORRUPTION IN THE WORLD TODAY

"Corruption has appeared in the land and the sea, on account of what the hands of men have wrought," it says in the Holy Quran (Chapter 30:41).

How true! Corruption prevails everywhere on account of men's evil doings. Their hands, in fact, have built their own doom, and never before has such prophecy been fulfilled any clearer than today.

The world today is so evil and corrupt that people do not pay any attention to the preaching of good. Their hearts, minds, and souls are all going after evil and bloodshed of each other.

There is no peace among men; hatred and disagreement are universal. A change of rulership must take place in order to save the nations from self-destruction. They (men) have corrupted the land and sea with all kinds of deadly arms— weapons of destructin which their hands have built.

They delight greatly in war but not in peace. Who then can enjoy peace in the midst of such a mad world? Who can be trusted? The alarm of war is heard and possibly designed to wipe mankind from the face of the earth. The land is charged with every type of man-made weapon of destruction of each other's lives. The sea is filled with deadly surface ships and undersea crafts (submarines). The sky has been filled with planes loaded with death to drop on our fellow-men. Yet they (men) say PEACE! Where is any peace with such evil forces free to spread death and destruction on the poor innocent human beings of the earth? They glory in killing and are not satisfied with the prosperity they have enjoyed. Their thanks to God is to destroy His people. These evil people have worked all of their lives making trouble, causing bloodshed among the peaceful people of the earth and themselves.

Their (this evil people's) greed in ruling the black people of the earth is unequaled. They send all their armed forces against you to make you bow to their rule. Even in your own home they want to rule according to their desire and not to yours, although it your HOME.

Once they have access to enter your house, they will go to war with you before they will leave in peace. They will take over your property and call it theirs. "Allah will scatter them who delight in war." (Psalm 69:30)

Let the world ponder — what does history show that the white man can call his own outside of Europe? However, they spread out and into the homes of black mankind of the earth, taking by armed force the black people's homes and making slaves of them for many centuries.

The day has arrived for all corruption to end. It is the Day of Allah and the people of Allah (believers in Allah) must have peace. The troublemakers must be punished and brought to an end so they will never be able to give trouble anymore.

THIS OLD WORLD IS A GREAT TROUBLEMAKER

This (old) world killed my people (mentally) and did them injustice. She must now, therefore, be destroyed. She is a great troublemaker and will not accept the New World. She prepares to go to war against it (the New World) and against the righteous Ruler.

DESTRUCTION OF THE PRESENT WORLD

Allah has warned us of how He would (one day) destroy the world with bombs, poison gas, and finally fire that would consume and destroy everything of the present world. Not anything of it (the present world of white mankind) would be left. Those escaping the destruction would not be allowed to take anything of it out with them.

Allah (has) pointed out to us a dreadful looking plane in the sky that is made like a wheel. It is a half-mile by a half-mile square; it is a human-built planet. (I won't go into all of the details here, but it is up there and can be seen twice a week; it is no secret.) Ezekiel saw it a long time ago. It was built for the purpose of destroying the present world. Allah has also hinted at plaguing the world with rain, snow, hail and earthquakes.

THE "TIME OF THE DEAD"

The Bible says, "Behold, I (Allah) make all things new." (Rev. 21:5)

Then it says, in Rev. 11:18, "Will the Old World accept the New? No, the Old World will not accept the New. Therefore, the Old one must be destroyed. And the nations were angry, and Thy wrath is come, and the Time of the Dead, and (Thou) shouldest destroy them which destroy the earth (black people)."

Never was this Scripture so plainly fulfilled as it is being fulfilled today!

The nations are angry and warring against each other—over who shall rule the other—and over what part of the earth they shall possess. Yes, it is the TIME OF THE DEAD (the mentally-dead, or the so-called Negroes) and time that they should be judged (be given justice).

THE COMING OF A NEW WORLD

It is necessary for me to consult or refer to the Bible for this subject. It can be found in the Holy Quran, but not in the exact words as they are found in the Bible.

Another reason why I have to quote from the Bible, here as elsewhere, is that my people (the so-called Negroes) know or read no Scripture other than that (Bible). Besides, they don't even understand the Bible—though they read and believe in it—and it is my duty to awaken them from it, because it is surely the graveyard of my people.

(There are, of course, many Muslims who don't care to read *anything* in the Bible. But those Muslims have not been given my job and, therefore, I ignore what they say or write pertaining to this matter.)

Now, it says in the Bible: "Behold, I (Allah) make all things new; and He said unto me, 'write, for these words are true and faithful'." (Rev. 21:5) This refers to the coming of a NEW WORLD, or a NEW order of things.

It does not take a wise man to see the necessity of a new order of things or a NEW WORLD, since the old one has fulfilled its purpose. Let the Christians' preachers now ponder: If the time comes when Allah (God) will make all things NEW, will the Christians as we see them today be in that which Allah (God) will make NEW—after the destruction of the wicked and their kingdom and world? Just when should the end of the old world be? The exact day is known only to Allah, but many think that they know the year.

"WHAT'S INSIDE OF THE DOOR OF THE NEW WORLD?"

The teachings of both the Bible and the Holy Quran and all the prophets take us only up to the door of the New World and do not make us qualified members to be received on the inside (of that door).

On the inside of the door of the New World is that which no eye has seen and no ear has heard. Nor has it entered the heart of man to know what Allah has prepared for those who serve Him.

THE SO-CALLED NEGROES WILL BUILD THE NEW WORLD

The New World (of Truth, Freedom, Justice and Equality) will be built by the so-called Negroes. Allah (God) Himself has chosen them to do so.

A people that was no people—the rejected and despised—shall soon be known as the builders of a great New World!

ISLAM WILL BE THE NEW WORLD'S RELIGION

There are many—other than the devils —who are actually ignorant of the fact that Islam of the New World will (also) be a "New Islam." For there are some practices of it (today's Islam) that won't be necessary in the New World

THE NEW WORLD WILL MAKE THE SO-CALLED NEGROES A NEW PEOPLE

The so-called Negroes will be the beneficiaries (of the New World), for they, too, will be made "New" by Allah. They will take on a new growth—spiritual as well as physical—and will become the most beautiful, the most wise, the most

powerful and the most progressive people that ever lived!

MUSLIMS ALONE WILL RULE THE NEW WORLD

The white Christians think that they and their religion will be the rulers in the New World. Followers of many other religions think the same. But they will be greatly surprised and disappointed, for Allah has rejected all religions except Islam.

Muslims alone will rule the New World, and this generation will live to witness the change.

Lift up your heads, my people! Shake off the Old World of evil and put on the "New" garments of the New World's Righteousness!

AS LONG AS YOU STAY ASLEEP ....

The time Allah (God) had given the devils to rule the world (6,000 years) was up in 1914. But as long as you stay asleep from lack of Knowledge about yourselves, you are extending their time (of their life). They can continue to live only as long as you remain mentally dead to the knowledge of yourself and the devils.

Chapter Seven:

Babylon and America

THE SINS OF BABYLON

What were the sins of ancient Babylon?

According to history, Babylon was rich and very proud, and her riches increased her corruption.

She had every merchandise that the nations wanted or demanded. Her (Babylon's) ships carried her merchandise to the ports of every nation.

She (Babylon) was a drunkard. Wine and strong drinks were in her daily practice. She was filled with adultery and murder. She persecuted and killed the people of God. She killed the saints and prophets of Allah (God). Hate and filthiness, gambling and sports of every evil dominated the life of all Babylonians.

"Babylon is suddenly fallen and the destroyed howl for her; take blame for her pains, so she may be healed." (Jer. 51:81)

AMERICA AND ANCIENT BABYLON

I compare the fall of America with the fall of ancient Babylon.

America's wickedness (sins) is the same as the history shows of ancient Babylon. Only America is modern and much worse.

AMERICA IN THIS TIME AND DAY

All nations are charged with committing fornication with her (America) and are now angry with her. The merchants of the earth were made rich in trade with her.

America, the richest of all countries, pays the highest wages; she must therefore charge a high price for her merchandise; and those who buy her merchandise for resale must sell for a profit, and they too are thus made rich from such deals.

They shall weep and mourn over her (America), for no man buyeth her merchandise anymore (Rev. 18:11). When people are rich and powerful, they can't see themselves being brought to aught overnight.

Who can remain in power if God has decided against him? "He (Allah) exalts whom He pleases, and whom He pleases He brings to an aught," it says in the Holy Quran.

THE EVILS OF AMERICA

I warn my people (the so-called Negroes of America) to let the destruction of Babylon serve as a lesson for them.

The white people (of America) have gone to the limit in doing evil, and as God (Allah) dealt with ancient peoples, so will He deal with modern Babylon (America).

AMERICA IS FALLING

America is falling, my people. She has to fall, because she is a habitation of devils and every uncleanness and hateful people of the righteous. Forsake her and fly to your own—before it is too late.

You of my people that believe, write to me and get your name on the Nation's Book of Life (Islam).

ALLAH WILL CUT OFF THE BREAD OF AMERICA

God says, "Son of Man, when the land (people) sinneth against Me by trespassing grievously, then will I stretch out My hand upon it, and will break the staff of bread thereof, and will send famine upon it, and will cut off man and beast from it." (Ezekiel 14:13)

Today we see it with our own eyes, but the wicked Americans are too proud to confess that they see the bread of America gradually being cut off. Take a look into the Southwest and Midwest, and see the hand of Allah (God) at work against modern Babylon—to break the whole staff of her bread for her evils done against His people (the so-called Negroes).

Texas and Kansas were once two of the nation's most proud states—Kansas for its wheat and Texas for its cattle, cotton, corn and many other vegetables and fruits. Recently these two states were in the grip of a drought and continuous raging dust storms. Their river beds lay bare, their fish stinking on the banks in dry parched mud. When the rain came, it brought very little relief and did more damage than good. Snow came—and it brought not joy but death and destruction. And after the snow came more dust storms, and then more rain, with hail stones.

America has not seen the large hail stones; one day she will see hail stones the size of small blocks of ice breaking down crops, trees, the roofs of homes, and killing cattle and fowls. Behind this there will be terrific earthquakes, frightening and killing more people. Sickness and death will be widespread. She (America) is getting a token of it now.

Chapter Eight:

Fear

POSSESSOR OF KNOWLEDGE NEED NOT FEAR

It is natural for one to fear that of which he has no knowledge. However, when Truth and Knowledge are made clear to you, as is being done today through the teachings contained in this book, you have no cloak for fear. Your mixing up of truth with falsehood is only because you fear your enemies (the devils).

WE MUST NOT FEAR ANYONE EXCEPT ALLAH

Allah (the Almighty God) doesn't care for us when our fear for Him is less than that for our enemies (the devils).

We must not fear *anyone* except Him (Allah).

Allah says: *"Me, and Me alone should you fear. Believe in that which I have revealed, verifying that which is with you, and be not the first to deny it; neither take a mean price for my message; and keep your duty to Me and Me alone."* —THE HOLY QURAN 2:40-41.

THE FEAR OF LOSING JOBS AND POSITION

The fear in the so-called Negroes has now increased to the point where they fear of not being given work to make an honest living. The slavemaster is practicing this scheme of fear on the so-called Negroes (who accept Islam) on certain government jobs to frighten them (from accepting Islam).

It is one of the slavemaster's main tricks—to keep the so-called Negroes from their salvation in Islam. But they (the so-called Negroes) should be wise to this old-time trick.

The clergy and the educated class of my people also have the fear of losing their present position and false respect of the slavemaster. But such people are mentioned as going to hell with the beasts (Rev. 19:20), and they must and will be made to acknowledge the Truth— for the slavemaster will soon be forced to give them up (Rev. 20:13).

THOSE WHO FEAR AND UNBELIEVERS WILL SHARE PUNISHMENT

It's a shame to see our people in such fearful condition. "The fearful and the unbelieving shall have their part in the lake which burns with fire and brimstone which is the second death." (Rev. 21:8)

The devil whom they fear more than Allah (God) was not able to protect himself against Allah. His (the devil's) followers, therefore, shared with him the fire of hell. Though they had suffered one death (mental death) already, by fearing the devil and rejecting the Truth they suffered another (physical death), which was the final death.

The devils know that they have deceived the world with their false religion (Christianity). Consequently, they are so afraid that Islam is going to give life and light to the so-called Negroes that they sit and watch over them day and night.

LEAVE CHRISTIANITY, FEAR WILL LEAVE YOU

Once the so-called Negroes drop the religion of slavery (Christianity), and accept Allah for their God and His religion (Islam), Allah will remove their fear and grief, and they will not fear nor grieve any more.

WHAT OUR ENEMY IS DOING

The enemy is alert, wide-awake and ever on the job to prevent the so-called Negroes from believing in Allah and the True Religion of Allah and His Prophets —the Religion of Islam. The enemy is well-aware that Allah is the Rock of our Defense and Islam is the House of our Salvation.

Fear is the worst enemy that we (the so-called Negroes) have, but entire submission to Allah and His Messenger will remove this fear. The white race put fear in our foreparents when they were babies, so says the Word of Allah.

The poor (so-called) Negroes are so filled with fear of their enemy that they stoop to help him against their own salvation.

Beware of what you are doing lest you be the worse loser. If they had only been taught the TRUTH, they would act differently.

THERE CAN BE NO LOVE FOR AN ENEMY

It is against the very nature of God, and man, and all life, to love their enemies. Would God ask us to do that which He Himself cannot do? He hates His enemies so much that He tells us that He is going to destroy them in hell-fire, along with those of us who follow His enemies.

Chapter Nine:

Freedom, Justice and Equality

IT IS NATURAL TO LOVE FREEDOM AND JUSTICE

It is entirely natural for man to want to be equal of man. It is natural, again, for man to love the Brotherhood of Man (except the man devil).

Further, it is natural for man to love FREEDOM for himself, for Freedom is essential to life, and to love JUSTICE for himself, for without Justice there is no joy in freedom and equality.

Can you say, my people, that you are enjoying freedom, justice and. equality in Christianity?

EQUALITY IN BROTHERHOOD

The Muslims make the so-called Negroes who believe in Allah and His religion of peace (Islam) EQUAL in the Brotherhood of our Nation.

Have the Christian (whites) done so, or are they doing so now—making the Christian believing so-called Negroes their equal brothers?

EQUALITY UNDER LAW

My people (the so-called Negroes) do not demand anything from the whites of this country, except that they stop killing them unjustly and give them equal justice under their laws as they do for themselves, and EQUAL WAGES as they do for their kind and for the same labor. They demand neither land for themselves, nor instruments and money to go elsewhere, which the whites have acquired from the so-called Negroes' labor, sweat and blood. No real civilized people would ask for such small pay in return for four hundred years of free labor, free blood, life and for the use (misuse) of their women by the devils at their will—only a foolish people without the knowledge of the white race and their own kind would accept that.

ISLAM RECOGNIZES EQUALITY OF BROTHER-HOOD; CHRISTIANITY DOES NOT

Islam recognizes complete equality of Brotherhood; a Muslim is truly the brother of another Believer, regardless of how black the skin or how kinked the hair. He is welcomed with sincere and open arms and recognized by his light-skinned or copper-colored Arab brother. He is also recognized in the same way by his brown or yellow-skinned Japanese, Chinese and Indian brothers. Can you say this for your Christianity, my people? No, your slavemasters' religion does not recognize equality of brotherhood.

In Islam, in fact, you are not a believer until you first love for your brother that which you love for yourself.

If the white Christians had meant good for you and me, why did they make slaves of us, and why are they still subjecting us to the most severe and ugliest injustices?

A SHOW OF TEMPTATION

These days America puts on a show of Temptation with her (white) women posing half-nude in the so-called Negroes' faces in the most indecent manner that is known to mankind. This you can see in any newspaper or magazine, and in the streets. The purpose of this Show of Temptation is to trick and drag the so-called Negroes to death and hell with them (the devils).

Be wise, my people, and shut your eyes at them. Do not look at them in such an indecent way. Clean your homes of white people's pictures, and put your *own* on the walls. The only so-called Negroes' pictures you will see in the white people's homes are those of ones they have lynched or they want to kill, and of those who betrayed their own people for them (the devils).

NO "INTEGRATION"

The slavemasters' children are doing everything in their power to prevent the so-called Negroes from accepting their own God and salvation, by putting on a great show of false love and friendship.

This is being done through 'integration' as it is called, that is, so-called Negroes and whites mixing together, such as in schools, churches, and even intermarriage with the so-called Negroes, and this the poor slaves really think that they are entering a condition of heaven with their former slave-holders, but it will prove to be their doom.

Today, according to God's word, we are living in a time of great separation between the blacks and the whites.

The prophesied 400 years of slavery —that we the so-called Negroes would have to serve (the white) people—ended in 1955. The so-called Negroes must now return to their own; nothing else will solve their problem.

The divine power is working and will continue to work in favor of the so-called Negroes' return to their own. The separation would be a blessing for both sides.

SEPARATION FROM THE SLAVEMASTERS IS A MUST

You, my people, must know that you have not been rightly civilized. No one can enslave another who has equal education (Knowledge). My people lack science (knowledge) of the right kind.

Allah (to Whom praise is due) is now here to give you and me a superior knowledge of things and a country to ourselves. Separation of the so-called Negroes from their slavemasters' children is a MUST. It is the only SOLUTION to our problem. It was the only solution, according to the Bible, for Israel and the Egyptians, and it will prove to be the only solution for America and her slaves, whom she mockingly calls her citizens, without granting her citizenship. We must keep this in our minds at all times that we are actually being mocked.

I think it is a DISGRACE to us for ever being satisfied with only a servant's part. Should not we, as a people, want for ourselves what other civilized nations have?

SLAVEMASTERS' EDUCATIONAL SYSTEM WON'T HELP US

Recently one of my people who is other than a Believer wrote to me and boasted about our "having some of the finest schools" and mentioned a few well-known names as "proof" of the "great progress" my people have made in America in recent years.

But is it not true, my people, that your schools, colleges and universities are from the slavemasters? And who is benefitted by the graduates of these schools — the white man or the so-called Negroes?

I say that regardless of how much education your slavemasters give you, if they never teach you a true knowledge of self, you are only a free slave to serve them or others than your own.

Is your present educational system getting you independence from the slavemasters' children? Is it or has it put the idea in your head to seek some of this good earth for you and your people who number over 17 million in America, and a place to call your own? NO!

Who appoints your men to degrees and scientists to high government posts? Is it not their white masters whom they are going to serve? You will seek white men's jobs, but not a country for your people.

DAYS OF JUDGEMENT AND SEPARATION OF PEOPLES

We are now living in the days of Judgement, and in the days of a great Separation of peoples and Nations. This problem of separating (the boundary lines of many nations are being removed) you and I from our enemies and placing us in our own land (back among our own people) will prove to be a great boon for us. It will help raise the so-called Negroes of America up to their proper place in civilization.

39

Chapter Ten:

The Hereafter, Heaven and Hell

THE HEREAFTER

What is meant by the Hereafter? It means, "After the destruction of the present world, its power and authority to rule." More specifically, it means, "After the present rule of the Man of Sin."

Some say that the Hereafter means "after the Judgement," that is, after the Man of Sin and his people have been judged and sentenced to death. I say that this present world was sentenced to death when the Man of Sin was made and all who follow him. It says in the Holy Quran (7:18), "Whoever of them will follow you, I will certainly fill hell with you all." The Bible says, "These both were cast alive into a lake of fire." (Rev. 19:20)

We all look forward to a Hereafter, to seeing and living under a ruler and a government of righteousness, after the destruction of the unrighteous.

The people of the Man of Sin (the devils) even are worried, disgusted and dissatisfied with their own world and wish to see a change to a better world; but they desire to be a ruler in that Better World too, which they wouldn't be permitted by Allah.

FOR MY FOLLOWERS, HEREAFTER IS NOW!

Everyone of us—the so-called Negroes —who accepts the religion of Islam and follows what Allah has revealed to me will begin enjoying the above (Hereafter) life here, now!

Yes, the glorious joy and happiness is yours for the asking, my people. Accept Islam and see your God in truth, and the righteous will meet and embrace you with peace (As-Salaam-Alaikum).

You will be clothed in silk, interwoven with gold, and eat the best food that you desire. This is the time when you enter such life, for your God is here in Person, and you will never be that which you cannot be any more, after believing in Him.

WHAT THE HEREAFTER WILL BE LIKE

The Righteous will make an unlimited progress in the Hereafter; peace, joy and happiness will have no end. Wars will be forgotten; there will be no place for disagreement.

The present Brotherhood of Islam is typical of the life in the Hereafter. The only difference is that the Brotherhood in the Hereafter will enjoy the spirit of gladness and happiness forever in the Presence of Allah.

There will be such a change in the general atmosphere of the earth (in the Hereafter) that the people will think it is a new earth. It will be the heaven of the righteous forever; no sickness, no hospitals, no insane asylums, no gambling, and no cursing or swearing will be seen or heard in that life. All fear, grief and sorrow will stop on this side as a proof.

The life in the Hereafter is an image of the spiritual state in this life. Just think how good you feel when in the Divine Spirit for awhile — you are so happy that you don't feel even the pain of sickness, no trouble or sorrow, and that is the way you will feel always in the next life.

HOLY QURAN ON THE HEREAFTER

The Holy Quran Sharrieff and the Bible are filled with readings on the Hereafter. Here I shall quote only these beautiful verses from the Holy Quran (89:27-30):

"O soul that is at rest, return to your Lord, well-pleased with Him, well-pleasing; So enter among My servants, and enter into My Paradise."

THE HEREAFTER IS NOT A LIFE OF SPIRIT

My people have been deceived by the arch deceiver in regards to the Hereafter. They think the Hereafter is a life of spirits (spooks) up somewhere in the sky, while it is only on the earth, and you won't change to any spirit beings. The life in the hereafter is only a continuation of the present life. You will be flesh and blood. You won't see spooks coming up out of graves to meet God.

Read the Scriptures carefully on the life in the Hereafter, and try to understand their true meaning, and you will find that the Hereafter isn't what you have been believing. My people, no one is going to leave this planet to live on another; you can't even if you try! You can't reach the moon and live on it. So BE SATISFIED and BELIEVE IN ALLAH, live where you are on this good earth, but BE RIGHTEOUS.

RESURRECTION OF THE DEAD

You, who believe literally in the physical resurrection of the dead, must remember the Bible (Rev. 14:4) teaches that the first righteous to be saved (the 144,000) are redeemable from among men, not out of the grave. It is a sin that you are so blinded that you cannot see, nor will you accept plain TRUTH. Surely, there is a resurrection of the dead. It is one of the principles of Islam, but not the physically dead in the graveyards. It is the mentally dead, the ignorant, whom the devils' falsehood has killed to the knowledge of truth, the DIVINE TRUTH. This TRUTH must now be preached to them to awaken them into the knowledge of Him again. You and I know that it can't refer to a physically dead person, because that has gone back to the earth, or up in smoke, or eaten by some wild beast or fish of the sea? What about the people who died before the Flood and after? Even Adam? They have nothing to rise from. Remember, the Old Testament (the Torah) dosen't teach of a resurrection of the dead, according to Job (chapter 7:9), wherein it says "He that goeth down to the grave shall come up no more." He must be right as we haven't seen one come up yet from the grave that was really dead. Surely, if it had meant a physical death God would have taught it to Adam, Noah, Abraham and Moses and all of the ancient prophets would have had a knowledge of it, even Job, but not so is the case.

THE DAY OF RESURRECTION IS HERE

The day of resurrection of the mentally-dead so-called Negroes has arrived.

Wake up, my people! You have lived overtime in bondage to the White Christians.

WHICH WAY LEADS TO HELL ?

The unbelievers of my people are often told by the slavemasters' children that if they accept Islam it would lead them to "hell."

They (the so-called Negroes) should know that if anything has led or will lead them to hell, it's the white (devil) race and their false religion (Christianity), and NOT Islam.

Islam is meant to elevate my people (the so-called Negroes) and to sit them in heaven; this the world shall soon know and believe.

HELL IS IN WHITE MAN'S CHRISTIANITY

I don't have to say to the so-called Negroes that hell is for them in white man's Christianity! They know it and have experienced it, in this Christians' hell.

FIREWOOD OF HELL

The true One God is Allah, the author of Islam.

The Holy Quran states that what you worship besides Allah is the Firewood of Hell.

WHAT SORT OF HELL ?

The Christians say, "Confess the Lord Jesus Christ or you (who are other than the Christians) will burn in hell forever." That hell must not be so hot that one can burn in it forever and never burn up.

IN HEAVEN OVERNIGHT!

If the so-called American Negroes would try living in unity, have love for self and their kind (the Black Man) they would be in Heaven overnight!

Chapter Eleven:

The Forbidden Foods

POISON FOODS

Allah (God) has blessed America (not because she is good) with plenty of good eatables — millions of pounds of beef, lamb, chicken and fish of all kinds are available at all times. Yet she eats the dirty and filthy hog, to Allah's dislike, and almost forces the so-called Negroes to eat it, or I would say everyone. America drinks more alcohol — forbidden by Allah—than anyone else. She is blessed with so much wheat that she can hardly find room to store it, and will even burn it to raise the price, yet she teaches the so-called Negroes to eat CORNBREAD and the HOG, both of which are a slow death to my people in the southern parts of this country.

My people have been reared on such POISON FOODS and now all the doctors in the world can't tell them that it is not good for them.

The hogs contain trichina (called pork worms) whose larvae infest the intestines and muscles of hog-eaters. This animal (hog) is one of Allah's most hated and it was never intended to be eaten.

THE HOG IS POISON!

Now of course, I do not care if *all* the white people eat the hog; I am only concerned with my people—the so-called Negroes—who don't know, nor do they understand. I know that not one of my poor people will go to Heaven (see the Hereafter) who eats this POISON HOG after being given the knowledge.

THE HOG IS NOT A FOOD

The hog (pig) was made for the white race and for medical purposes only; regardless of who eats it, I say that it was not made to be taken as a food. On this point Allah and His Prophets are my witness, and are with me.

BIBLE FORBIDS EATING OF HOG

The Bible forbids you to eat the hog, Mr. Christian. It is forbidden by God through the mouth of His Prophets. Do you think that you can clear yourself with God by eating the swine and claiming it is all right?

I will give here some of the places in your Bible where you can read of this Divinely-forbidden flesh (the hog). "Of their flesh shall you not eat, nor touch their dead carcass." (*Deut.*, 14:8) "I have spread out my hands all the day unto a rebellious people who eat swine's flesh and broth of abominable things is in their vessels." (*Isa*, 66:2) "In the heathen sacrifices some offered swine blood and burned incense to an idol." (*Isa*, 66:3) "They that sanctify themselves (call themselves sanctified and holy) in the Garden behind one tree (in the church behind its pastor) eating swine flesh, the abomination and the mouse, shall be consumed together, saith the Lord". (*Isa*, 66:18, where it also says: "Stand by thyself, come not near to me, for I am holier than thou." Such, of course, is said by hog-eating Christians!) Again it says in the same chapter: (66:5) "These are a smoke in my nose, a fire (anger) that burneth all the day."

In Mark, 5:11-16 it says: "Of their flesh thou shall not eat." Go and ask my followers who were one possessed with devil and the swine how they feel since their release from such by Allah, to Whom praises are due.

The POISON SWINE is a scavenger and lives and thrives on filth, and the tissues of the hog are swarmed with parasites and worms which are 99 per cent poison. Allah has said: "They shall not eat the Swine." Says He in the Holy Quran, Chapter 2:168, 169 and 173: "O men, eat the lawful and good things out of what is in the earth, and do not follow in the footsteps of the devils." (The devils referred to are not other than the white people who eat the hog and other things forbidden by Allah.)

The devils (referred to in the Holy Quran) only enjoin upon you evil and indecency, and that you may speak against Allah and that which you do not know. When it is said to the so-called

Negroes, "Follow what Allah has revealed," they say, "Nay, we follow what we found our fathers upon" — though their fathers had no sense at all, nor did they follow the right way. He (Allah) has only forbidden to you what dies of itself, and the blood and the flesh of the filthy swine, and that over which any other name besides Allah has been invoked.

Allah says that the Caucasian race, having once been a savage people living in the caves and hillsides of Europe, ate almost everything like meat and ate it *raw* for 2,000 years. That was, to be exact, in the years before 4000 B.C. Naturally, they know good but just don't have the nature to do good, and you can't make them good unless they are returned into that which they were taken from. *You*, my people, who have the Divine Nature of God, do the things that are right. So *Unite, live and die for each other in the name of Allah and His Religion of Peace, Islam.* Do not let the Caucasians attract you to the evil things that you see them doing.

MEDICAL SCIENCE ON HOG

The hog is called *khanzier* in the Arabic language, which means: *I see* (khan) and *foul and very foul* (zier). This animal is indeed so foul, ugly and filthy that it is known to the medical profession that eating it decreases the mental power. There is a small opening on the inside of its front legs out of which flows a mass of corruption. The Medical Science says of this: "The opening is an outlet of a sewer." (See *MONITOR OF*

HEALTH, by Dr. J. H. Kellogg, M.D.; pages 117-124).

The hog is completely shameless. Most animals have a certain amount of shyness, but not the hog, or his eater; they are similar. The hog-eater, it is a fact, will go nude in the public if allowed; his temper is easily aroused and under such conditions he will speak the ugliest, vilest, and most filthy language one has ever heard spoken in public. His mouth is full of cursing and swearing.

The hog is not a peaceful animal and can't get along in peace with others of his kind. He is the greediest of all animals. He will not divide his food with his young, except the milk in their bellies.

The hog is the cause, the very root of most of our sickness. STOP EATING IT and see for yourself.

THE HOG AND ITS EATERS

The white race knows that people eating swine flesh, committing acts of adultery, robbing, murdering and lying shall not be recognized as Servants of God and they won't see the Hereafter, unless, of course, they repent today. We see the white race in the South fighting to keep the so-called Negroes from even voting for one of their own (white people) to rule them.

They even fight their own laws to prevent the so-called Negroes from sitting in classrooms with their children, although it is better even for *us* to not allow ourselves to be destroyed by mixing with them. Get an equal education, but stay to yourselves today. It is too late in the evening to try mixing the races.

Chapter Twelve:

The Truth and Falsehood

KNOW THE TRUTH, MY PEOPLE !

Because my people, the so-called Negroes, know so little about themselves and know so little of the treachery of the many other racial groups, we suffer untold human indignities in order to obtain so-called "equality" of opportunity in public accomodations, schools, churches, sports, etc. We seek to be accepted as members of the white slavemaster's family. And regardless of the savage treatment we receive, we pour out our life-blood like water to be near our enemies. May Allah open my people's eyes that they may see and know the Truth!

If they only knew the Truth, they would prefer sitting as far removed from their enemies as the East is from the West.

Know the Truth, my people, and return to your God, Allah, and His Religion, Islam, that I may protect you and save you.

MIXING OF TRUTH WITH FALSEHOOD

The Holy Quran warns us against mixing the Truth with Falsehood. *"And mix not up the Truth with Falsehood,*

nor hide the Truth while you know." (Chapter 2:42)

But mixing up the Truth with falsehood is the policy of the devils, and nearly all the religious leaders of Christianity are guilty of it—because they don't know which is truth and which is falsehood.

The devils are really confused, thinking and planning against the truth and trying to hide falsehood.

TRUTH MUST TRIUMPH OVER FALSEHOOD

The Truth must triumph over falsehood, as day triumphs over night. When we deny the truth it shows that we love falsehood more than truth. If we fear to speak the truth for the sake of falsehood, that is not only hiding the truth but is actually showing fear and distrust in the Divine Supreme Being, His Wisdom and His Power.

This hiding and mixing the truth with falsehood because of fear of the enemy (devils) is taking a great number of our people to hell with the devils.

DID THE TEACHER TEACH THE TRUTH ?

The so-called Negroes are, as far as

their education and training is concerned, the product of the white people.

Now if they have been taught the Truth, why is it that the devils are afraid of my people believing that which is different from what they (the whites) taught them?

WHOM DID THE "GREAT DECEIVER" DECEIVE?

Think over the saying of the Bible, Rev. 20:3, 8: "The great deceiver of the nations."

Whom did the "great deceiver" deceive of my people? He deceived those (so-called Negroes) who had received his mark (the mark of Christianity—the Cross).

"THE DEVIL'S WAY"

It's the Devil's Way to bring the people of Allah (the so-called Negroes) in opposition to Him—by teaching them to believe and do just the thing that God forbids.

Muhammad (May the peace and blessings of Allah be upon him!), for instance, did not try making a likeness of God, nor have his followers ever tried to do so; he (Muhammad) and his followers accept and obey this law of Allah, the One God.

But not the Jews and Christians—they always preach and act against it, and teach others to do likewise.

THE DIVINE PURPOSE

Our slavery at the hands of John Hawkins and his fellow-slavetraders and suffering here in the Western Hemisphere for four hundred years was actually all for a Divine Purpose: that Almighty Allah (God) might make Himself known through us to our enemies, and let the world know the Truth that He alone is God.

THE KEY OF KNOWLEDGE

It is said—sometimes by the devils themselves—that the so-called Negroes educated and trained by the whites and their kind will never be able to maintain self-rule That is true.

But my people (the so-called Negroes) are now reaching out for Allah and Islam, and for training from others of their OWN NATION who are and have been independent long before the white race was even created!

Therefore, the KEY OF KNOWLEDGE that would make the so-called Negroes capable of self-government, which the white race has always held back from my people, will now be given to them (the so-called Negroes) by Islam.

Chapter Thirteen:
Islam and Muslims

ISLAM – THE RELIGION OF PEACE AND UNITY

Islam is the religion of Peace and it brings about great contentment and peace of mind in those who accept and follow it. Islam is also a unifying religion and its author is God (Allah) Himself. It teaches against the doing of evil of every kind, great or small.

ISLAM – THE RELIGION OF DIVINE POWER

Islam is a religion of Divine Power. It will give great power to the helpless so-called Negroes, to overcome the devils and their false religion, Christianity, which has never helped the so-called Negroes against the white Christians' brutality.

ISLAM IS OUR SALVATION

Allah (Himself) chose for us ISLAM as a religion.

ISLAM is our salvation. It removes fear, grief and sorrow from any believer and it brings to us peace of mind and contentment.

ISLAM – THE ORIGINAL RELIGION

Islam is the original religion of *all* black mankind. There is no doubt about it, according to the meaning of Islam and what the Holy Quran Sharrieff teaches us of it. Islam means peace and submission to the will of Allah (God), who is the Author of Islam.

ISLAM – THE RELIGION OF ALL THE PROPHETS

The name "Islam" is not an invented one, as is the case with other religions. The name of our religion comes from Allah Himself, and is the religion of all the Prophets of Allah, including Abraham, Moses, Jesus, and Muhammad, the Last of His Prophets. Says the Holy Quran, "Surely the True Religion with Allah is Islam."

ISLAM – THE RELIGION OF PEACE

Islam means peace, therefore it is the Religion of Peace. Could we imagine Allah giving mankind any other religion but one of peace? Or could we imagine a prophet of Allah bringing us a religion other than of peace? Certainly not.

ISLAM IN THE BIBLE

It is Islam, the Religion of Peace, and none other, that God offers us in the Bible (Num. 6:26; Ps. 29:11-85:8; and Is. 26:3-32:17). There are many other places in the Bible that prove that Islam, the Religion of Peace, is mentioned as being the religion of Allah (God).

ISLAM — THE RELIGION OF TRIBE OF SHABAZZ

The religion of the whole tribe of Shabazz was none other than Islam. It was also the religion of Yakub, the father of the white race, before his fall.

ISLAM — THE PERFECT RELIGION

Allah says of Islam in the Holy Quran, "This day I have perfected for you a religion; completed my favor on you and chose for you Islam as a religion." (Chapter 5:3)

"RIGHT RELIGION IN THE RIGHT STATE"

I have often used this expression, which is a quotation from the Holy Quran. I shall now explain what this expression exactly means:

A religion is in the "right state" when its author is the All-Righteous Being (Allah) and it is believed and practiced according to His will. It must also apply to our nature in which we were born. That, then, is the "right religion in the right state."

ISLAM ALONE CAN UNITE THE SO-CALLED NEGROES

It is a great job trying to change the so-called Negroes from the ways of their slavemasters and to unite them. It may take much suffering but I say that it CAN be done. Islam will unite us all. I know Christianity can't unite us; instead, it divides us. That is what it was intended to do, to divide people.

HOW ISLAM BENEFITS US

The religion of Islam makes one think in terms of self and one's own kind. Thus, this kind of thinking produces an industrious people who are self-independent. Christianity does just the opposite: makes the so-called Negroes lazy, careless and dependent people.

Think over such slavery teachings as this: "That a rich man can't see the hereafter," and compare it with the promise of Allah who offers the righteous Heaven (riches) while they are alive.

I must continue to warn you that you can't depend on the white race to care for you forever. There has got to be an end to your dependence on them. So, why not start in time seeking something for self? Know this, my people, that this is the fall and end of the white race as a dominant power on the earth, and that the loss of Asia (alone) to the white race means the end of their luxury.,

It must come to pass, believe it or not! So get on to your kind and be benefitted by Islam.

WHY ISLAM MUST OVERCOME OTHER RELIGIONS ?

The answer to this question is very simple: Because Islam is the only religion of Allah, and He (Allah) has declared (in the Holy Quran) that Islam MUST overcome all other religions which are not from Him.

It says in the Holy Quran, "Is it other than Allah's religion that they seek to follow, and to Him submits whoever is in the heavens and on earth, willingly or un-willingly." (3:82) We bear witness to the TRUTH that everything of Allah's creation obeys Him, regardless of size or numbers.

ISLAM IS AGELESS AND WILL LAST FOREVER

When Muhammad started teaching Islam in Arabia over 1300 years ago, just 600 years after the death of Jesus, he and his followers and successors almost converted the whole world back into Islam in a few hundred years. However, the re-conversion had to be slowed down to allow the devils to rule their time out. This has now taken place—the devils' time IS UP, and once again Islam is on the march, this time to never relax until all is under it or off the planet earth.

Not to mention the people of Gold Coast of West Africa only, but all black Africans are now turning to Islam. Go make an inspection for yourself, if you do not believe. Islam is now in America for the first time since the Red Indians

came here 16,000 years ago, and it is here for the acceptance of the so-called Negroes whose fathers were once Muslims in their original home and who now are the last members of that chosen people to hear Islam, the Religion of Allah.

WHITE RACE WILL NEVER ACCEPT ISLAM

The white race, by nature, can't be righteous. Islam was taught to them from Moses to Muhammad, but they were never able to live the life of a Muslim believer and can't do it today. This fact the so-called Negroes must learn about the white race. They must learn that the white race cannot be righteous unless they could be born again (grafted back into the black man).

The poor, blind, deaf and dumb so-called Negroes work hard and live in hope that some day the white race will treat them right but this will never come to pass. And if they ever do treat them right, it will be against the will of that people. Certainly they can do it against their will but how long can such insincere love and justice last?

WHY NOT ISLAM FOR ALL MANKIND ?

The answer to this question ("Why not Islam for all Mankind?") is simple: All mankind can't believe and obey the teachings of Islam. All mankind are not members of the Righteous. Islam is righteousness and he who would believe in it and do the Will of Allah (God) must be by nature one born of Allah. The only people born of Allah is the Black Nation of which the so-called Negroes are descendants. That is why Islam is offered to them.

THE LIGHT OF ISLAM WILL SHINE FOREVER

"They desire to put out the light of Allah with their mouths, but Allah will perfect His light though the unbelievers may be averse," it says in the Holy Quran (61:8).

It means that regardless of the efforts (of the devil) to put out the light of Truth (Islam) today, it will continue to shine the world over, and forever!

ISLAM WILL REPLACE ALL OTHER RELIGIONS

"He it is who sent His Apostle with the guidance and the True religion that he make it overcome the religions, all of them, though the polytheists may be averse." (The Holy Quran, 61:9)

In the above verse Allah (God) in the last days of this present world (of wicked infidels) states that He must destroy false religions with the True Religion— Islam. It (Islam) must overcome all other religions.

That also means, as is indicated by the true meaning of the above verse, that Allah in the judgement of the world will definitely NOT RECOGNIZE any religion other than Islam.

Take to task all the learned teachers of religions and they will admit that God IS One and that He will have only one

religion in the Hereafter—Islam—which will replace all other religions.

ALL OPPOSITION TO ISLAM WILL VANISH

Search the Scriptures of the Bible and Holy Quran, and these will tell you that ultimately all opposition to Islam will vanish.

There are today two major religions which are opposed to the religion of peace, Islam. These are Buddhism and Christianity. With the help of Allah, these two opponents of Islam will be so completely eradicated from the planet earth that you won't even find a trace of them.

I say that Christianity is *already* dying a natural death.

ISLAM, AND NOTHING ELSE BUT ISLAM!

Why do I stress the religion of Islam for my people, the so-called Negroes?

First, and most important of all: Islam *is* actually *our* religion by nature. It is the religion of Allah (God) and not an European-organized white man's religion.

Second: It is the original, *the only* religion of Allah (God) and His prophets. It is also the only religion that will save the lives of my people and will give them divine protection against our enemies.

Third: Islam dignifies the black man. It gives him the desire to be clean, internally and externally, and to have, for the first time, a sense of dignity.

Fourth: Islam removes fear and makes one FEARLESS; it educates us into the knowledge of God and the devil, which is so necessary for my people.

Fifth: It makes us to know and love one another as never before.

Sixth: Islam destroys superstition and removes the veil of falsehood. It heals us both physically and spiritually by teaching what to eat, when to eat, and what to think, and how to act.

Seventh: It is the only religion that has the Divine power to unite us and save us from the destruction of the War of Armageddon, which is now. It is also the only religion in which the Believer is really divinely protected, and the only religion that will survive the Great Holy War, or the final war between Allah (God) and the devil.

I say, therefore, Islam and nothing else but Islam is meant to solve the so-called Negroes' problems and raise them from their mentally-dead condition. Islam, in fact, will put the black man of America on top of the civilization.

prophets, we make it a heaven. If we follow and obey the devil and his prophets, we make it a hell.

Islam brings about a peace of mind and contentment to the believer, and for the first time, love for our own black brothers and sisters. What one loves for himself, he must love for his brother. I will say here that this alone is salvation to you and me, just learning to love each other as brothers. Islam, unlike Christianity, is doing this right *in your midst*.

Regardless to how long and how hard you try to be a good Christian, you never have a sincere, true love for your own black brother and sister as you should. Islam will give you true brothers and sisters the world over, and this is what you need.

A people subjected to all kinds of injustices need to join Islam, as you are sure of Allah's help in Islam. Why don't the preachers of my people preach Islam? If they would, overnight they could be on top.

OTHER NOTABLE ASPECTS OF ISLAM

There are, of course, many other notable and worthy aspects of Islam my people should know about.

Islam, for instance, makes hell and heaven not two places but two *conditions of life*, which is very easy to understand. For there could never be either unless it was brought about by our own efforts or making. The earth is our home and we can make it a hell or heaven for us. If we follow and obey Allah and His

PRINCIPLES OF BELIEF IN ISLAM

Every Muslim is required to do the following:

1. Keep up prayer.

2. Spend of what Allah (God) has given him in the cause of Truth (Islam).

3. Speak the truth regardless of circumstances.

4. Keep himself (or herself) clean, internally and externally, at all times.

5. Love his brother (or sister) believer as himself (or herself).

6. Be kind and do good to all.

7. Kill no one whom Allah has not ordered to be killed.

8. Set at liberty the captured believer.

9. Worship no God but Allah.

10. Fear no one but Allah.

The above are the teachings of the Prophets.

ISLAM'S NUMBER ONE PRINCIPLE OF BELIEF

Belief in the One God, Allah, is the Number One principle teaching of Islam.

Muslims know and believe that Noah, Abraham, Moses and Jesus, and all the prophets of Allah also believed in the One God and taught this Truth.

SELF-DEFENSE IN ISLAM

The Holy Quran forbids "compulsory conversion" and teaches that a Muslim should never be the aggressor "but fight in the way of Allah with those who fight against you" (Chapter 2:190).

THE SIGNS OF ISLAM

Islam is most surely the "right religion in the right state." Here is another proof:

Islam uses for its Signs the Sun, Moon and the Star. These three elements (of Nature)) are most essential for our well-being, and they represent a physical work of Freedom Justice and Equality.

CHRISTIANITY, BUDDHISM AND ISLAM

What a difference there is between the three religions!

The first teaches that there are three Gods, not one. It also requires worship of Mary, mother of Jesus, and of the desciples of Jesus. The second, Buddhism, requires belief in "re-incarnation," and contains many ignorant practices.

Islam, on the other hand, is entirely free of confusing doctrines and of ignorant practices.

It (Islam) teaches an eternal heaven for the righteous. (Hell, according to Islam, is not eternal.)

It (Islam) also teaches that if a brother kills a brother the murderer must be killed, or anyone that murders a Muslim (must be killed).

HINDUS ARE ENEMIES OF ISLAM

The true religion of Allah and His Prophets Noah, Abraham, Moses and Jesus was Islam, and it is to overcome all religions. *"He (Allah) it is, who sent His Apostle with the guidance and the true religion, that he may make it overcome all other religions, though the Polytheists may be averse"—THE HOLY QURAN 61:9.* That is why the white race and Indian Hindus have always been and are now the enemies of Islam and Muslims.

MUSLIMS

Believers in ALL of the Prophets of

God and the Scriptures—Torah, Bible, Quran—are referred to as Muslims.

The Muslims make (recognize) no difference in any of the Scriptures as long as these are from Allah.

They (Muslims) believe in Moses and Jesus, also the true Scriptures that these two prophets brought to their people.

NATION OF ISLAM WILL LIVE FOREVER!

There is no end to the black nation (Islam). That nation is to live forever. But the so-called Negroes don't know it, and their slavemasters know that they don't know it and, therefore, have them (the so-called Negroes) deceived one hundred per cent.

MUSLIMS SHOULD BE PROUD OF THEMSELVES

The Muslims should be proud of themselves and of their black skin and kinky wool, for this kinky woolly hair will be the future ruler (Dan. 7:9 and Rev. 1:14).

MUSLIMS PRAY TO ALLAH, NOT MUHAMMAD

We Muslims love all of Allah's prophets. But we will not pray for life to come to us from a dead prophet—not even Muhammad, who lived nearly 1,400 years ago. We pray in the name of Allah, and mention the name of His Last Prophet in our prayer as an honor to him and as our thanks to God (Allah) for His last guide to us.

NO MUSLIM SHALL SPEAK ILL OF ANOTHER

I am not surprised at what the disbelievers (devils) think and say of me. However, when a supposed Brother Muslim joins the disbelievers in (differing from and criticizing) what I write, then I am surely surprised. No Muslim should speak ill of another, especially when they lack correct information about the one they speak of. I know that no TRUE MUSLIM *does* or *will* speak against another to delight the disbelieving people.

If your door today is open to all peoples, which include human devils whom Allah is angry with and whom He threatens with total destruction, I leave it over to Him (Allah) to judge between you and me.

THE FAITHFUL'S MARK

To be truthful with you, God has said to me, He will not accept any white people in His Kingdom. A special Mark will distinguish the righteous from the devils, and it will be in their foreheads caused by prostrating. The Muslims prostrate in their prayers on rough floors or rugs, which produce a mark on their forehead. (Some of my followers have such a sign now, produced by the five-prayers-a-day obligation.) The righteous is always marked by his righteousness, as the wicked is marked by his or her wicked acts. They are

54

actually marked by nature and are recognized by both parties.

OVER ONE BILLION MUSLIMS

The true believers of Islam equal in number that of the total population of the whites on our planet (400,000,000). However, by nature *all* members of the black nation are Muslims (lovers of peace), and thus they number well over the one billion mark.

MUSLIMS IN U. S. PRISONS

I receive many letters from inmates of jails and correctional institutions across the country. They are from so-called Negroes who want to accept Islam.

For their benefit I write here that they should send us their slave names and we shall add these to those of other Muslims registered with our Temples of Islam. Later on, as soon as they are free, they should report to the nearest Temple of Islam in person and formally join on to their own Holy Nation of Islam.

Anyone who desires to accept Islam, however, must pledge to serve and obey Allah and His Apostle.

ISLAM IMPROVES PERSONALITY

Islam changes the believer in every respect, into a better person, and makes evil hateful to him. It also manifests that which is in us, whether good or evil (even that which we didn't know was in us).

MUSLIM NAMES ARE BEAUTIFUL

All Muslim names are beautiful and have a beautiful meaning. Ninety-nine per cent of them are divine attributes (of Allah). Remember, my people, Jones, Johnson, Smith, Hog, Bird, Fish, Bear, Woods, and such names as Roundtree will not be accepted by Allah, your God and mine.

Chapter Fourteen:

Women and Children

OUR WOMENFOLK

We must learn to respect, love and protect our womenfolk.

There is no nation on earth that has less respect for and less control of their womenfolk as we the so-called Negroes here in America. Even the animals and beasts and fowls of the air have more love and respect for their females than have the so-called Negroes of America.

Our women are allowed to walk and stay in the streets all night long, with any strange men that they desire. They are allowed to frequent any tavern or dance hall that they like, and whenever they like. We allow them to fill *our* homes with children who are *other than our own* —children who are often fathered by the devil himself. Then when the devil man decides to marry one of our women the so-called Negro press and magazines will make it their front page news, but the white press hides it. The white press will not print anything about a so-called Negro man marrying into the white race, but you seem to think it is an honor to your own Nation when your daughter goes over to your enemies, the devils.

Our women have been used and are still being used by the devil white race, ever since we were first brought here to these shores as slaves. Our women can't go out without being winked at, whistled at, yelled at, slapped, patted, kicked, and even driven around in the streets by your devil white enemies right under your nose and in your eyesight, and yet you do nothing about it, nor do you even protest it.

WE MUST CHANGE OUR WOMEN'S PRESENT CONDITION

Even today we allow the white race to slap, shoot and kill our women—just as they did over three hundred years ago. This shameful condition must be changed, and real soon.

But, my people, you simply can't control or protect your women from the enemies as long as you are in the white race's false religion called Christianity. This religion of theirs gives you no desire or power to resist them (your enemies—the devils). The only way and place to solve this problem is in the Religion and Nation of Islam.

Islam will change the present condition of our women *overnight*.

DO YOU HATE YOURSELF AND YOUR KIND?

Do you hate yourself and your kind?

You might say, "No". But that's just what you show to the world—that you hate yourself and your kind—when you hate and reject your own women for those of the devil race and desire to dissolve yourself into their (white) race, regardless of how much that race hates you and your people.

(And then you think the white race should recognize you as their equal! Let us not fool ourselves. There are many places here in America where the white race doesn't think you are clean or intelligent enough even to use their rest rooms!)

OUR MEN ARE TO BLAME FOR THE WOMEN'S CONDITION

Our (so-called Negro) women fill themselves and you with social diseases of the devil white race. Neither you nor she is wanted in the society of the intelligent people.

Who is to blame for her condition? It is YOU MEN who are to blame, not women. It is you, the men, and not women, who are the heads of your families.

PROTECT YOUR WOMEN!

Protect your women, my people, as other nations protect theirs. Take your women out of the arms of the slave-masters' children and all strange men—at any cost—and put a stop to this freedom of their mixing with whom they please. Why should your women want their enemies?

PROTECTION OF OUR WOMEN IS IMPERATIVE

We protect our farms by pulling up weeds and grass by the roots and by eliminating destructive animals and birds, also by poisoning the insects that threaten to destroy our crops, so that our harvest might be bountiful. Yet how much more valuable should be our women, who are our fields through whom we produce our Nation! Shouldn't we then protect them from all strangers and our enemies? Is it not essential that we preserve our Nation and keep it as pure as Almighty Allah (God) gave it to us in the Beginning?

I say that protection of our women is all-important and imperative.

The white race doesn't want us to destroy it by intermarrying with their kind; they will shoot and kill you to protect their women. Can you blame them? No. Blame your foolish self for not having enough respect for your own kind and your own Nation to do likewise.

PRACTICAL STEPS FOR THE SAFEGUARD OF OUR WOMEN

We must stop our women, at once, from imitating the white race, from trying to look other than their own kind, by bleaching, powdering, ironing and coloring their hair, painting their lips, cheeks, eyebrows, wearing shorts, going half-nude in public and going swimming on beaches with men.

If you must have swimming pools, have separate and private ones for your women, and guard them from all men.

Stop your women from going into bars and taverns and sitting and drinking with men and strangers. Stop them from sitting in those places with *anyone*, for they shouldn't even *be* there.

Stop them also from using unclean language in public as well as at home, and prevent them from smoking and drug addiction habits.

EDUCATION AND TRAINING OF CHILDREN

You must teach and train your boys and girls in your *own* schools and colleges. And keep your little children, especially your little girls, from mixing with white children. When you do this, then your own people who are the Original People of the Human Family will respect you as a Nation.

LEARNING IS A VIRTUE

The education and training of our children must not be limited to the "three Rs" (reading, 'riting and 'rithmetic) only. It should instead include the history of of the black nation, the knowledge of civilizations of man and the Universe, and all sciences. It is necessary that the young people of our Nation learn all they can. Learning is a great virtue and I would like to see all the children of my followers become possessors of it. It will make us an even greater people tomorrow.

"M. G. T."

The Muslim girls of our Nation should spare no effort to learn their special duties and responsibilities as future wives and mothers. The University of Islam in Chicago and the one in Detroit are both equipped to give them the finest training in their special fields. Those who are unable to attend one of these schools should take advantage of the instruction available in the Temple of Islam M. G. T. (Muslim Girls' Training) classes.

Chapter Fifteen:

The Bible

THE BIBLE HAS BEEN TAMPERED WITH

The religious leaders of Christianity have mixed up the Truth of the Bible (with falsehood) so much that they admit someone has tampered with the book. The Bible now teaches both *against* evil as well as *for* evil. For instance, it says that we should not drink strong drinks; wine is prohibited in some places and in other places it says that it is good for us.

THE BIBLE'S TEACHINGS

I do not know of any scriptural book or religion that does not contain some good. What Allah demands today-is a book or religion that is *all* good, not a mixture of truth and falsehood, not a book or religion that is or has been tampered with by His enemies.

The Bible is called a Holy Book, and is often referred to as the Word of God. The present English edition is said to be translated out of the original tongues into the present English language by the authority of one King James in 1611.

What is the original tongue or language that the Bible was written in? What language did Moses speak? Originally, the Torah (Old Testament) was given to Musa (Moses) in 2000 B.C., who spoke ancient Egyptian Arabic, and the second half (New Testament) was revealed to Isa (Jesus) 2000 years ago, and he (Jesus) spoke both Arabic and Hebrew.

From the first day that the white race received the Divine Scripture they started tampering with its truth to make it to suit themselves and blind the black man. It is their nature to do evil and the book cannot be recognized as the pure and Holy Word of God.

The Bible is now being called the *poison book* by God Himself, and who can deny that it is not poison?

It has poisoned the very hearts and minds of the so-called Negroes so much that they can't agree with each other.

The Bible opens with the words of someone other than God trying to represent God and His creation to us. This is called the Book of Moses and reads as following: "In the beginning God created the Heaven and the earth." (Gen. 1:1) When was this beginning? There in the Genesis the writer tells us that it was 4,004 B.C. This we know, now, that it refers to the making of the white race, and not the Heaven and the earth.

The second verse of the First Chapter of Genesis reads: "And the earth was without form and void; darkness was upon the deep and the spirit of God moved upon the face of the waters." What was the water on, since there was no form of earth? As I see it, the Bible is very questionable.

After God had created everything without asking for any help from anyone then comes His weakness in the 26th verse of the same chapter (Genesis). He invites us to help Him make a man. Allah has revealed that it was *us* that was invited to make a man (white race). A man is far more easy to make than the Heaven and the earth. We can't charge these questionable readings of the Bible to Moses because he was a Prophet of God and they (Prophets) don't lie.

If the present Bible is the direct Word of God, why isn't God speaking rather than His Prophet Musa? Neither does Moses tell us here in the first chapter of Genesis that it is from God. No, we don't find the name Moses mentioned in the chapter.

The Bible is the graveyard of my poor people (the so-called Negroes) and I would like to dwell upon it until I am sure that they understand that it is not quite as holy as they first thought it was.

I don't mean to say that there is no truth in it. Certainly, plenty of truth, *if understood*.

Will you (the so-called Negroes) accept the understanding of it?

The Bible charges all of its great Prophets with evil, it makes God guilty of an act of adultery by charging Him with being the father of Mary's baby (Jesus); again it charges Noah and Lot with drunkenness and Lot getting children by his daughter.

What a poison book!

We, being robbed so thoroughly of the Knowledge of self and kind, are opposed to our own salvation in favor of our enemies, and I here quote another poison addition of the slavery teaching of the Bible: "Love your enemies, bless them who curse you, pray for those who spitefully use you, him that smiteth thee on one cheek offer the other cheek, him that taketh (robs) away the cloak, forbid not to take (away) thy coat also." (Luke 6:27-29)

The slavemasters couldn't have found a better teaching for their protection against the slaves' possible dissatisfaction with their masters' brutal treatment.

Christianity is a religion organized and backed by the devils for the purpose of making slaves of black mankind.

Freedom, Justice, Equality; money, good homes, etc.—these Christianity cannot give us (not the Christianity that has been taught us).

Allah has said that Christianity was organized by the white race and they placed the name of Jesus on it being the founder and author to deceive black people into accepting it.

Our first step is to give back to the white man his religion, Christianity, church and his names. These three are chains of slavery that hold us in bondage to them. We are free only when we give up the above three.

The Bible, church and Christianity have deceived the so-called Negroes. I pray (to) Allah to give them life, and light of understanding.

THE BIBLE ON THE DEVILS

In the Bible, 1 Thessalonians 3:14-16, St. John 8:44-48, 2 Thessalonians 2:3, 4, 7-12, and 1 Corinthians 10:21—all refer to the white race and their kind as the real devils, who even killed Jesus and the Prophets before him, and who persecute us who believe and preach the Truth of Jesus and his religion.

Chapter Sixteen:

My Mission and Objective

MY MISSION

I have been risen to raise my people here (the so-called Negroes), and to help them into the knowledge of Self, and their God Allah (who is in Person among them) and the devils (their open enemies).

MY OBJECTIVE

I am doing all I can to make the so-called Negroes see that the white race and their religion (Christianity) are their open enemies, and to prove to them that they will never be anything but the devils' slaves and finally go to hell with them for believing and following them and their kind.

DIVINE PROTECTION FOR MY PEOPLE

Islam is being offered to the so-called Negroes of America for the sole purpose of bringing them into the knowledge of Truth.

Another purpose is to give them Divine protection, and to set them on top of civilization (this is mentioned in the Bible if you can understand).

Without Islam the so-called Negroes would never become a free, independent people under those who had enslaved them. It's Allah's doing and we can't hinder Islam's progress here.

THE AIM OF ISLAM IN AMERICA

The aim of Islam in America is:

(1) To teach our people (the so-called Negroes) the Truth;

(2) To clean them up and make them self-respecting and to unite them on to their own kind;

(3) To bring them face to face with our God, and to teach them to know their enemies.

In short, Islam is offered to our people (the so-called Negroes) as a *Remedy of their Ills*, or as a Solution to their problems.

WHAT HINDERS THE PROGRESS OF ISLAM IN AMERICA

The greatest hindrance to the progress of Islam in America is the so-called Negro Christian preacher, ever-preaching the same old falsehoods, singing and mourning over the air, calling on a dead Jesus and a mystery God that doesn't even exist.

The so-called Negroes were born in such falsehoods and made to fear them by the Slavemasters—lest they should not be fed, clothed or sheltered.

WE ARE SURE OF OUR WORK AND SUCCESS

We are sure of our work and success. When we get through opening the so-called Negroes' eyes, the white Christians will take their hats off to them.

I DO NOT MAKE MISTAKES

I do not make mistakes in what I write pertaining to these two races—black and white—and I do not need to study the theory of evolution to learn about them...

Theories do not always prove to be the truth. I have the truth from the All-Wise One (Allah), to Whom praise is due. He has raised the curtain of falsehood which kept the true knowledge of the black and white races (especially the white race) from the peoples of the earth for 6,000 years.

They say that I am a preacher of racial hatred, but the fact is that the white people don't like the truth, especially if it speaks *against* them. This we have known all our lives.

"WHAT HAVE I DONE?"

This is a question often asked of me or of my followers by those who are not the Believers.

I am doing that for thousands (of my people) which Christianity failed to do —that is, uniting the so-called Negroes and making them to leave off evil habits that the preachers of Christianity have not been able to do for a hundred years. We offer that in Islam what Christianity offers beyond the grave.

THE KEYS OF GOD

I am very insignificant in your eyes, my people, but I have the Keys of God to your (so-called Negroes') problems, and you should not fear, for the DAY has come that you will have to seek refuge in the "New World" (of Allah), which is something far better and more enduring than the white race's Christianity.

Chapter Seventeen:
The Muslim Prayer

MUSLIM'S PRAYERS

Muslims pray five times a day, not once a week or once a year.

They pray at sunrise, at noon, at mid-afternoon, at sundown, and before retiring.

If awakened through the night, another prayer is made! In fact, two prayers should be said during the night, making a total of seven prayers a day.

There is no worship of a Sunday or Sabbath in Islam, all the days are worship days.

The Muslims wash and clean all exposed parts of their bodies before each prayer, which is made facing in the direction of the SUNRISE (East).

MUSLIM PRAYER SERVICE IS UNEQUALED

Study the Muslim's way of worship and you will agree with me that there is no better way of divine worship. Why? For one thing, the Muslim always washes and cleans himself before communicating with Allah (God). In other words, he first cleans his own body and *then* invites the clean Holy Spirit to come (into his body). That is the best state (of body as well as of mind) in which to say one's prayers.

MUSLIM PRAYER SERVICE BEST SUITS THE SO-CALLED NEGROES

I say that no religious worshipper could beat such a preparation for his prayer service or use more honor and submission to his Maker as I have described in preceding paragraphs.

The Muslim's Prayer Service, therefore, is the best to be used by the so-called Negroes in America, for its words fit *their* condition more than any other people on earth.

Until now, we have been turned from our God (Allah) towards the devil, believing in and worshipping a trinity of Gods, with our faces down or upward towards the sky, and our thoughts of God in the sky.

DESCRIPTION OF PRAYER

The Muslim begins his prayer by declaring that ALLAH IS THE GREATEST and that he bears witness that there is "No God but ALLAH," and that none deserves to be served (worshipped) but Him. He further declares that Muhammad is His Apostle (an Apostle whom Allah would raise from the lost and found people of the seed of Abraham in the Days of Judgement).

After this the Muslim declares: "I have turned myself to Allah, being upright to Him who originated the Heavens and the Earth. I am indeed not one of the polytheists." (A polytheist is one who believes in more than one God.)

MEANING OF THE VARIOUS "STEPS" OF MUSLIM'S PRAYER

The various "steps" of the Muslim's prayer — turning, bowing, sitting, and prostrating—all have a beautiful meaning, which space won't allow me (to explain) here.

The Muslims are in accord with the whole Earth's turning; the Earth revolves on its axis eastward toward the Sun, being attracted by it. Eastward is where we look to daylight, and it is in that direction wherefrom came the Prophets and civilization of man.

Again, it is the East from which direction we were told to expect the coming of the Son of Man (God in Person) in the last days of the wicked.

MUSLIM'S OFT-REPEATED PRAYER

The Muslim's oft-repeated prayer is as follows:

"In the Name of Allah, the Beneficent, the Merciful. All Praise is due to Allah, the Lord of the Worlds; the Beneficent, the Merciful; Master of the Day of Requital. Thee do we serve, and Thee do we beseech for help.

Guide us on the Right Path — the path of those upon whom Thou hast bestowed favors, not of those upon whom Thy wrath is brought down, nor of those who go astray."

Through this beautiful prayer the Muslim seeks the Path to trod that will bring him Divine help, and for the so-called Negroes ISLAM is that path which will get Divine help on their side.

My people, set your face upright for the religion in the right state—Islam!

THE SIGNIFICANCE OF THE SEVEN PRAYERS

The Muslim is required to pray five times a day, and twice at night if he awakens. This totals seven. What is the significance of this number seven?

Do we not have seven inhabited planets? And a Seven-thousandth year after the six thousand years of the devil's rule?

Are we not reminded of this in the six work days of the week (the six thousand years of the workings of the devils) and the seventh to rest which belongs to the Lord (the original owners, the Black Man)?

ABLUTION

The process of bodily cleanliness which precedes the Muslim's prayers is known as Ablution. Here is how it is performed:

The Muslim first washes his hands, then he rinses his mouth. Then he washes his arms, up to the elbows (if exposed). Ablution is completed by washing the feet.

THE SIGNIFICANCE OF ABLUTION

Each part of the Ablution requirement has some significance. For instance, the Muslim washes his hands to "get rid of any evil" they might have commited. This also signifies that the Muslim thus asks Allah to wash his hands in the Spirit of Forgiveness.

OBJECT OF MUSLIM'S PRAYER

The object of Muslim's prayer is the purification of heart, which is necessary for spiritual advancement.

BENEFIT OF PRAYER

Allah promises many blessings to you if you turn to Him in prayer. Nations are no doubt destroyed when they indulge in evil inordinately, and they prosper only so long as their good qualities preponderate.

THE HOLY QURAN ON PRAYER

"So bear patiently what they say, and celebrate the praise of the Lord before the rising of the sun and before its setting, and glorify (Him) during the hours of the night and parts of the day, that thou mayest be well pleased." (THE HOLY QURAN, 20:30)

"Keep up prayer from the declining of the sun till the darkness of the night, and the recital of the Quran. Surely the recital of the Quran at dawn is witnessed." (THE HOLY QURAN, 17:78)

"Say: Call on Allah or call on the Beneficent. By whatever name you call on Him, He has the best names. And utter not thy prayer loudly nor be silent in it, and seek a way between these." (THE HOLY QURAN, 17:116)

"Recite that which has been revealed to thee of the Book and keep up prayer. Surely prayer keeps (one) away from indecency and evil; and certainly the remembrance of Allah is the greatest (force). And Allah knows what you do." (THE HOLY QURAN, 29:45)

MECCA, THE HOLY CITY

When the Muslim has performed his Ablution, (which means also that his hands are now spread forth, his ears cleaned from the hearing of evil, and eyes closed from seeing evil,) he then steps on his prayer rug or mat, and faces toward the ONLY HOLY SPOT on our planet— the Holy City of Mecca.

Chapter Eighteen:

The Holy Quran

THE GLORIOUS HOLY QURAN SHARRIEFF

The book that the so-called American Negroes (Tribe of Shabazz) should own and read, the book that the slavemasters have but have not represented it to their slaves, is a book that will heal their sin-sick souls that were made sick and sorrowful by the slavemasters.

This book will open their blinded eyes and open their deaf ears. It will purify them.

The name of this book, which makes a distinction between the God of righteous and the God of evil, is: Glorious Holy Quran Sharrieff. It is indeed the Book of Guidance, of Light and Truth, and of Wisdom and Judgement.

But the average one should first be taught how to respect such a book, how to understand it, and how to teach it. The Holy Quran Sharrieff contains some of the most beautiful prayers that one has ever heard recited or read. It is called the Glorious Quran and without mistake that is just what it is.

This book, the Holy Quran Sharrieff, is not from a prophet but direct from Allah to Muhammad (may peace and the blessings of Allah be upon him!) not by an angel but from the mouth of Allah (God).

And Allah is the Great DISTINGUISH-ER between Truth and falsehood in the judgement of the world, of whom the enemy of truth has ruled the nation of black mankind with falsehood for the past six thousand years.

This book, the Holy Quran Sharrieff, pulls the cover off the covered and shows the nation for the first time that which deceived 90 per cent of the people of the earth without the knowledge of the deceiver.

The Revelation of the Book is from Allah, the Mighty, the Knowing One. And the Book (Holy Quran Sharrieff) is indeed a Guide unto the righteous because the All-Knowing-One and Best Knower has revealed it; and who knows better than Him as to what is best for every living thing?

Man makes himself a fool to try attacking Him (Allah) in arguments. So we have no doubt the Holy Quran Sharrieff is from Allah, the Lord of the worlds. It is one of the clearest-reading books you have ever read.

The God that revealed the Holy Quran Sharrieff to Muhammad (may the peace and blessings of Allah be upon him!) is the same that revealed the scriptures to the other prophets, according to the Holy Quran, which says, "Surely we have revealed to you as we revealed to

Noah and the prophets after him; and we revealed to Abraham, Ishmael, Isaac, Jacob, the Tribes, Jesus, Job, Jonah, Aaron, and Solomon; and we gave to David a scripture; and to Moses Allah addressed His words speaking to Him; and we sent Apostles we have mentioned to you before, and Apostles we have not mentioned to you." (4:163,164)

The Holy Quran's readings are not the kind that will lull one to sleep, but to get a real Holy Quran one should know the Arabic language in which it is written. As for translations, you can find a good one of it by Maulana Muhammad Ali and one by Allama Yusuf Ali.

A FEW TEACHINGS OF THE HOLY QURAN

Let us take a look at the opening of the second chapter of the Holy Quran. Here Allah addresses Himself to us as being the Best Knower and that we must not entertain any doubts about the purity of His Book (the Holy Quran).

"I am Allah, the Best Knower. This book, there is no doubt in it, is a guide to those who guard (against) evil," it says.

Allah Himself speaks in the Holy Quran, not like the Bible which mentions 'Thus says the Lord'.

In the Holy Quran, Allah challenges the disbelievers of our people and the devils combined to produce a chapter or

even a verse like it. I quote another verse of the same chapter (2:285): "The Apostle believes in what has been revealed to him from His Lord, and so do the believers; they all believe in Allah, His Angels, His Books, and His Apostles; We made no difference between any of the Apostles; and they (the believers) say, we hear and obey, our Lord; Thy forgiveness do we crave, and to Thee is the eventual recourse."

Can the proud Christians say with truth the same? No, they don't believe in Allah, not to mention His Prophets and the Scriptures of the Prophets, and they like to make a difference in the prophets. All the old prophets are condemned as being other than good, but Jesus they go to the extreme in making him a Son of God and (even) finally God. Yet they (also) say that they killed Jesus 'the Son of God' because he made himself the 'Son of God.'

THE 112th CHAPTER OF THE HOLY QURAN

We are today being brought face to face with Allah (God) for a showdown between Him and that which we have served as God beside Him. The lost and found members of the Asiatic nation are especially warned in the 112th Chapter of the Holy Quran against the worship of any God other than Allah, for it is Allah in person who has found them among the worshippers of gods other than Himself.

Chapter Nineteen:

Prophecies and Warnings

WHY PEOPLE REJECT A MESSENGER OR REFORMER

According to the past histories of prophets and reformers, the very people to whom they were sent with the light of Truth were their rejecters and even their enemies. Why is this so? It's because some people do not appreciate a change in their life, though it may be for their own good. They look at prophets and reformers with suspicion, in doubt to that which is other than what they have been believing all their lives.

The people of Noah, Abraham, Moses and Jesus were in doubt as to what those prophets brought to them from Allah (God), until Allah brought about a showdown between the two.

The so-called American Negroes are also acting in like manner. They are so gravely deceived by the white man's Christianity and Bible that they doubt everything that doesn't have the white man's approval. But the time for a change has arrived and the so-called Negroes must be awakened to this fact.

WHY WE SUFFER PERSECUTION AND RIDICULE

My followers and I have spent and are spending much time and money, and we are suffering much persecution and ridicule, to awaken our people to the knowledge of their own Salvation. We also know that our present suffering is nothing compared to the joy that awaits us.

END OF THE FOOLISH ONES

The foolish ones, highly educated in ways other than those of Allah, become rich and powerful. Then they begin to *make* and worship gods which are the work of their own hands!

Even when the fools, who do not believe in Allah being the One God, are asked as to who made the heavens and earth, most surely they reply: "God." They would not and do not say, "God, the Son and the Holy Ghost." Then why do they not serve and obey God (Allah) alone?

The fools know better but won't admit it!

But end of such foolishness, and of those who practice it, is now at hand, and soon the world will witness it.

THE PROPHESY ABOUT THE 144,000

It is written (Rev. 14:1) that only 144,-000 of us will accept and return to our

God (Allah) and the rest, 16,856,000, would go down with His enemies. For this sad prophecy of the loss of my people, I write what I am writing, hoping perhaps that you may be able to beat the old prophets' prediction by making the truth so simple that a fool can understand it.

You must be rightly civilized. You must go back to you OWN PEOPLE and COUNTRY, but not one of you can return with what you have. You must know that this is the Time of Judgement of this World (of the Caucasian race) that you and I have known. Therefore, Allah has said to me that the Time is ripe for you and me to accept our own (the whole Planet Earth).

What are YOU waiting for—the destruction? Come, let us reason together. (But *you* cannot reason until you have a thorough knowledge of self). Who are you waiting on to teach you to the knowledge? (The white man's civilization will never work for us.)

A PROPHESY

Christianity, or the Christian world, does not care for the true religion (Islam) because her nature is against truth and justice.. Besides, white Christians fear (losing) their slaves (the so-called Negroes).

The Christians today are watching all the so-called Negroes to see which ones of them believe in the Truth (Islam) that Allah has given to me for my people. But all of them would wish that they were Muslims before it is over.

The Christians desire to put out the light of Allah with their (lying) mouths, but little do they know of Allah's own plans. "*Allah will perfect His light though the disbelievers may be averse*"—*THE HOLY QURAN 61:8.*

ENEMIES OF ISLAM BETTER WATCH OUT!

A prominent white Christian from the state of Georgia had recently insulted me and the whole Nation of Islam by threatening to drive us (the Muslims of America) into the ocean for teaching the so-called Negroes their *own* religion. He also said that America was a white Christian nation, that it was founded by "white man, *for* white men," and that they (the founders) never intended for America to fall into the possession of a dark race.

But why is it, then, that the white people (Christians) are hindering my people (the so-called Negroes) from going back to their own Religion and People, especially when they (the devils) are not going to divide this country with them and not going to treat them as their equal?

Moreover, the Bible teaches that one day "every man will turn and go to his Own." Did the white race originally own this part of our Planet? Aren't the red Indians the original owners (of it), who are brothers of the dark nation (of Islam)? There is no part of our Planet, in fact, that belongs or was ever given to the white race; the whole Planet belongs to us—the Nation of Islam!

The prominent white Christian from the state of Georgia and all his brothers (enemies of Islam) should, therefore, know that if they attempt to drive Islam into the ocean, the devils would themselves fall backward into a lake of fire.

69

THE THREAT OF AN ATOMIC WAR

America also faces the threat of an atomic war between the nations of the earth.

Yet my people (the so-called Negroes) have their eyes closed at the manifest judgement of Allah (God) going on in their midst to bring this country to nought.

ENGLAND'S POWER WILL DWINDLE

England has lost and still is losing her power over the world of black mankind. Her power will continue to dwindle, until she is left a mere stump of her power in what is called the British Isles.

THE RIGHT PATH FOR MY PEOPLE

It has been seen from the little chance my people have had to get a little education and they have shown and proven that they ARE the ORIGINAL PEOPLE, who are only asleep and in great need of the right civilized man who will perform his duty of awakening them. The so-called Negroes' fear of being deprived of food, clothing and shelter, also the usual smile of the white slavemasters' children prevents them from seeking the true knowledge of their own nation's civilization.

I say that they MUST drop the slavemasters' names and religion, because both of these mean nothing but continued slavery. If they would understand, there is no other RIGHT PATH for my people.

Of course, some (not all) preachers and politicians, who live off the ignorance of their people, are opposed to the right civilization of our people (the so-called Negroes). These are the people who teach the so-called Negroes to eat the wrong food and to drink, to indulge in games of chance (gambling), to go half-dressed, and to look for salvation *after death* (and not give a hoot for salvation in *this life*, as right civilization teaches us). Their teachings, my people, are not for your good.

Come and follow the Right Path and the RIGHT GUIDE, and be rightly civilized.

JUDGEMENT OF THE WORLD

The judgement of the world has arrived and the gathering together of the people is now going on.

Why should there be a judgement of the world? Why was there a judgement of the people of Noah and Lot? The Bible says: "That day shall not come except there come a falling away first, and the man of sin revealed, the son of Perdition" (II Thessalonians 2:3).

The whole world of our kind awaits the awakening (to the knowledge of the good that is being carried on for their deliverance), and our awakening is the last step in the Resurrection and judgement of the world.

The end of the world has arrived and most of us know it, and our enemy's greatest desire is that we remain asleep.

Chapter Twenty:
Words of Advice to My People

WORDS OF ADVICE TO MY PEOPLE

I advise you, my people, that, first of all, you will never be able to live as you desire — in freedom, justice and equality—until you are in your own (Islam).

Whatever profession or trade you may have, do something for yourself and your kind and choose for yourself the one religion (Islam). Islam alone will secure for you favor and protection of Allah, also universal Brotherhood.

Stop looking for anything after death —Heaven or Hell. These are in *this* life. Death settles it all.

Stop eating yourself to death by eating three meals a day. Eat once a day and eat the best food, which when eaten correctly, keeps you in the best of health. Stay away from the HOG meat. Don't eat stale beef, chicken or fish. Eat fresh products.

Don't eat field peas such as brown or black-eyed peas and lima beans. Don't eat collard greens, cabbage sprouts, cornbread. Eat brown bread (whole wheat) and butter, if not over-weight, and a little cheese. Drink milk. Cook your food well done.

Pray five times a day with your face toward the east.

Love your black brother as thyself. Do good to all.

COME UNDER THE CRESCENT OF ISLAM!

Islam is the religion of peace and security. So why don't you accept it as *your* religion?

Come down off the Cross and get under the Crescent of Islam which will give you Freedom, Justice and Equality.

We are a Nation within a nation. Do we want respect as others? First respect yourself; only then others will respect you.

LEAVE YOUR FALSE PRIDE NOW AND ACCEPT ALLAH

Are you proud to submit to Allah (God) and sit in Heaven while you live, and have His protection against your open enemy? Then that is false pride and you should lose no time in shedding it. Take it or leave it, but you will soon wish that you had submitted to Allah. God is drying America up by degrees, little by little, and hell is kindling up. Islam *is* the right way for you, so join up the Brotherhood now.

INVITATION TO BLACK PREACHERS OF CHRISTIANITY

The poor black preachers (of Christianity) are really pitiful, to see how they are blinded and chained by the slavemasters hand and foot. They can't speak nor agree with truth even if they wanted to.

Come to me, my brother preachers, and believe in Allah, the true God, and His true religion, Islam, and free yourselves from such chained slavery.

LET US ALL UNITE UNDER THE CRESCENT!

Let us all unite and be One People, at peace with each other under the Crescent of our religion, Islam, and seek for *our* Nation what others seek for their Nation —a country to ourselves where we can live in unity, harmony and peace, away from our enemies.

NOTHING IN A NAME?

Some of the so-called Negroes are ignorant to the important advantage of having their own nation's names. They think there is nothing to a name. I say they are right, but only in regard to the names they are NOW using, and not in regard to their own nation's names which they don't have. The Bible says, "A good name is better than gold." To continue to bear the slavemasters' names makes them the property of their slavemasters and they can never hope to receive equal recognition in the civilized world.

PEACE AND HAPPINESS

The peace and happiness can't come to us under any other flag but our own.

If God desires for us such joy, why shouldn't we give up begging and be real men, and sit with the rulers of the earth, ruling our own?

HOME OF YOUR OWN

I want to see you, my people, in a country that you can call your own and where your highly trained and educated men and women can be benefitted. May Allah and Islam give it to you. There is no hope for such under the slavemaster's children and their flag.

HELP ME TO HELP YOU

Help me to get the message (of Islam) to our people (the so-called Negroes) with whatever cash that you are able to give, for it takes a lot of it to put this work over. But remember, you will get from two to ten for one. The whole earth will be given to you to rule forever. So help yourselves to escape out of America. She is falling . . . falling . . .!

Chapter Twenty-One:

Miscellaneous

IS THERE A MYSTERY GOD?

Who is the MYSTERY GOD? We should take time and study what has and is being taught to us. Study the words "Mystery God" and examine them, and if it be the Truth, lay hold to it.

To teach people that God is a "Mystery God" is to teach them that God is UNKNOWN. There is no truth in such a teaching. Can one teach which he himself does not know?

The word "Mystery," according to the English dictionaries, is: "something that has not been or cannot be" or "something beyond human comprehension." The unintelligent, or rather ones without divine knowledge, seem to delight themselves in representing that God is something mysterious (UNKNOWN). I say that such teaching makes the prophets' teaching of God all false.

According to Allah, the origin of such teaching as a mystery God is from the devils; it was taught to them by their father, Yakub, 6,000 years ago. They know today that God is not a mystery, but will not teach the Truth about it. He (devil), the god of evil, was made to rule the nations of earth for 6,000 years and naturally he would not teach obedience to a God other than himself.

So, a knowledge of the true God of Righteousness was not represented by the devils. The true God was not to be made manifest to the people until the God of evil (devil) had finished or lived out his time which was allowed him to deceive the nations. (Read Thessalonians 2:9-10 and Rev. 20:3-8-10).

The shutting up and loosening of the devil mentioned in Rev. 20:7 could refer to the time between 570 and 1555 A.D. when John Hawkins (and others) deceived our foreparents in Africa and brought them into slavery in America. That's nearly 1,000 years that they and Christianity were bottled up in Europe by the spread of Islam by Muhammad (may the peace of Allah be upon him!) and his followers (Muslims).

Their being loose to deceive the nations of the earth would refer to the time 1555 to 1955 A.D., during which they were loose (free) to travel over the earth and deceive the people.

Now their (the devils') freedom is being interfered with, by the Order and Power of the God of Righteous through the Nation of Righteous.

JOHN HAWKINS, THE ENGLISH SLAVE-TRADER

The problems of our people (the so-called Negroes) began four hundred years ago, from the day that our forefathers set the soles of their feet on the soil here in the Western Hemisphere, in the days of John Hawkins, the English slave-trader.

In the year 1555 when he (John Hawkins) began bringing our people away from our Native Land and away from our own people, to sell us to his white brothers in the West as merchandise for their slave markets, little did he realize at that time that by bringing us here as slaves he was actually sentencing his white brothers here to their doom, for the evil that they have since done to us and are still doing cannot be forgiven.

"JESUS" THE SHIP

John Hawkins brought our forefathers here (from Africa) on a ship named 'Jesus'; when this ship was on its way back for another load of our people, our foreparents stared at the old slave ship as it departed and begged to be carried back, but to no avail, and they said that "you can have this new Western world but give us the ship Jesus back to our people and country," which now has become a song among our people, which goes something like this: "You-can - have - all - the - world - but - give-me - Jesus."

But our foreparents did not know at that time it would be 400 years from that day before the real ship (God Himself) would come and get them and their children and cut loose every link of the slave chain that holds us in bondage to

our slave-masters by giving us a true knowledge of self, God and the devil and wipe away the 400 years of tears, weeping, mourning and groaning under the yoke of bondage to the merciless murderers.

WHAT OUR POOR ENSLAVED FOREFATHERS DIDN'T KNOW

Our poor black mothers and fathers, who were deceived by this devil John Hawkins' lies and empty promises, didn't have the slightest idea that their coming here to be sold into slavery would create a problem or problems that would take Almighty Allah (God) Himself and the Righteous Nation of Islam to solve. Nor did they (our poor black mothers and fathers) know that our problems wouldn't be solved until the end of the time of their arch-deceiving enemies (the devils).

SLAVE-NAMES

Allah has told us that we must give up our slavenames (of our slavemasters) and accept only the name of Allah (Himself) or one of the Divine attributes. We (the so-called Negroes) must also give up all evil doings and practices and do (only) righteousness or we shall be destroyed from the face of the earth.

SLAVERY AMONG THE ARABS

The Arabs are alleged to have slaves. The Arabs will answer for themselves, but I do know that no Muslim will enslave a Muslim. All Muslims are the brothers of another Muslim.

Any so-called Negro who turns Muslim can go and live among the Muslims of Arabia or anywhere on the planet earth and will be accepted as a brother and citizen of that government. Try it for yourself, brother. ALL ARE EQUAL IN ISLAM, not like your proud white Christians.

JEWS, OR HEBREWS

Believers in Musa (Moses) and the Torah are referred to as Jews or Hebrews.

The Jews or Hebrews believe that Musa (Moses) was a Jew, who brought them the Torah.

ABRAHAM AND ISHMAEL

Mecca is the Holy City wherein Abraham had made an attempt to sacrifice his son Ishmael, under a trial of Allah (God), which was also a sign of what would take place in the Last Days on finding and returning the lost-found people of Abraham and his son, Ishmael.

THE PARABLES OF LAZARUS AND THE RICH MAN

Remember the Bible's parables of Lazarus and the rich man, and Abraham acting as the spokesman for Lazarus? Abraham

knew that Lazarus would have been foolish enough to try making an attempt to save his master who was in hell to his own destruction. Not one time did the rich man ask Abraham to bring him water, but he knew the weakness of his servant Lazarus, and was fully aware of the consequences of Lazarus' attempt to aid him after being engulfed into the Divine chastisement.

NEBUCHADNEZZAR AND BELSHAZZAR

What does the Bible teach us were the sins of Nebuchadnezzar and Belshazzar that God disgraced and broke up the power of one and outright killed the other (Belshazzar)? Was it not for those (stolen) silver and golden vessels that were the property of the Temple of God?

It is the Temple's property now (the so-called Negroes) that God is after today. Nebuchadnezzar was charged with bringing them (the silver and golden vessels) from their Temple of God; so is England today charged with bringing into America the first black people to be sold into slavery.

MUHAMMAD THE PROPHET

Muhammad, an Arab, was a member of the black nation.

The Jews and Christians are of the white race, and they don't believe in Muhammad as a prophet of God. Naturally they don't believe in the Scripture

75

(of Muhammad) — The Holy Quran—
that Allah revealed to him.

The Arabs or Muslims have tried and
are still trying to get the white race to
believe and recognize Muhammad as a
Divine Prophet of Allah and the Quran
a Divine Revelation, as they recognize
Musa (Moses) and Isa (Jesus) and the
Bible coming from Allah (God).

The Holy Quran was revealed to Muhammad in the seventh century A.D.,
over 1300 years ago, who spoke Arabic.

The Holy Quran—it is holy because
it is the Word of Allah (God), who
speaks directly to His servant (Muhammad). 'Holy' means something that is
PERFECTLY PURE, and this we just
can't say of the poison Bible. Al-Quran
means, according to the scholars of the
language in which it is written, *that
which should be read*. It was revealed
(to Muhammad) in the month of Rama-
dan (2:185).

THE BLACK STONE AND
ITS SIGNIFICANCE

Remember Muhammad's finding of the
Black Stone out of its place, and inviting
the (four) Chiefs from four divisions to
come forward and take hold of each corn-
er of the mantle and help lift it (the
stone) into its *proper* place? That,
my people, was a sign of you and I here
today.

We need the help of our people who
are living in the four major points of our
compass to come and help raise us—their
dead brothers—and put us back into our

place, in our own Nation among our own
people in our own Native Land.

TOO MANY GODS ?

Some of my people say that "the
trouble with us is that we have too
many Gods." Then why not believe in
One God (Allah) and we all will be
trouble-free?

THE 1957 CONVENTION

We had a wonderful time at our Muslim convention (February 24-26, 1957)
in Chicago. We are sorry if you didn't
attend it, but plan on being with us
next February 26.

Nearly three thousand people attended
the Convention, of which two thousand
were Muslim delegates of my followers
from every state in the Union. There
was no smoking, drinking, weapons or
disputes among them—a true example of
brotherhood and peace as never witnessed before among persons who have been
said to be the "worst of mankind." It
was a wonderful sight of unity to behold.
All praise is due to Allah.

Since the Convention, new members are
registering with the Temples of Islam by
the dozens. We hope you, too, will join
up soon, if you haven't done so already.

THE YEAR 1914

We all know that 1914 was the year
that marked the end of the time (6,000

years) that was given the old world of the devils to rule.

HEAVEN ON EARTH

He (Allah) has made it clear what constitutes heaven on earth: Freedom, Justice, Equality; money, good homes and friendship in all walks of life.

PHARAOH

Remember the disgrace suffered by Pharaoh and his people for their opposition against Moses and his followers, just because Pharaoh feared that Moses would teach the people the true religion—Islam? Pharaoh set his whole army against Moses only to be brought to aught.

Pharaoh had deceived his slaves in the knowledge of Allah and the true religion (Islam), and indirectly had them worshipping him as God.

PHARAOH AND HIS SLAVES

The white people do not want their poor black slaves (the so-called Negroes) to leave this country and return to their Native Land and People. No—not any more than Pharaoh wanted to see his slaves leave Egypt. But Allah is going to take theirs (the devils'), as He took Pharaoh's slaves, believe it or not.

RECOGNITION AND RESPECT

White man's Christianity has abso-

lutely failed to get recognition and respect for us (the so-called Negroes). It has failed to get us recognition and respect even from those who *taught it to us.*

PEACE OF MIND AND CONTENTMENT

I say that all so-called Negroes should give up the white race's religion (Christianity) and come into their own (Nation of Islam). In Islam alone they will enjoy brotherly love, peace of mind and contentment.

GHANIANS AND THE SO-CALLED NEGROES

It is a joy to us to see our people in Ghana, Africa, get their independence, as you ought to be seeking yours instead of integrating, since your number is three times the population of Ghana.

Look at your brothers in the Sudan. You outnumber them too.

Where is your independence in these forty-eight states? But you don't love to be independent unless your white man is the boss.

THE POPE OF ROME

The white Christians falsely say and teach that their religion is from Jesus. In reality, it's from the Pope of Rome who is the head of the Church, and not Jesus. The blinded, deaf and dumb of my people, therefore, can never hope to

77

be successful with their white enemies being their religious heads and guides.

the lost Nation of Islam in the wilderness of North America.

LYNCHING AND BURNING

Isn't it true that white Christians in our South lynch and burn their black Christian believers?

Has anyone ever seen or heard of we Muslims lynching or burning the so-called Negroes who believe *or don't believe* in Islam?

PREACHER OF CHRISTIANITY

The greatest hindrance to the truth of our people is the preacher of Christianity. He won't accept it, nor is he content to let others alone who are trying to accept it. He is the man who stands in the way of the salvation of his people and as soon as people awaken to the knowledge of this man in their way to God, freedom, justice and equality and stop following him, the sooner they will be in heaven while they live. The preachers are afraid of the truth.

THE LOST-FOUND NATION

Allah greatly rejoices over us and is real happy that He has found us—

BEST CITIZENS

Despite the unfavorable attitude of those in power (Government) toward my followers, I must emphatically deny their being "subversive" in any way or manner whatsoever. How could anyone expect trouble of any kind from a peace-loving people who aren't even allowed to carry a pen-knife on them at any time?

My followers, in fact, are the BEST CITIZENS this country has got, because they are believers in Islam, the Religion of Peace, and in Righteousness, not evil, and they can do no wrong to anyone.

DECORATE YOUR HOMES WITH DIVINE ELEMENTS

Many of my people who are not the believers wear the Cross of Christianity around their necks or hang it in the bedrooms of their homes "for blessings." What sort of blessing can be expected from a symbol of death and destruction, which is the Cross?

My people, you should wear a Muslim "National" and decorate your homes with the flag of Freedom, Justice and Equality and *Divine* elements such as the Sun, Moon and Star.

Chapter Twenty-Two:

The Supreme Wisdom

THE SUPREME WISDOM

I have already explained in the first few chapters of this book who my people (the so-called Negroes) really are, who the devil (Man of Sin) is, and how the white people have been able to keep us in mental bondage to their kind for four hundred years—through the slavery teachings of Christianity.

I have also stated plainly just what constitutes Freedom, Justice, and Equality; Heaven and Hell; and the Hereafter. You don't find the true teachings of these in the Bible ("Poison Book"), except what suits the wicked slavemasters' purpose and desires. That's why I have to emphasize everything I say or write, even say a few things many times over, because my teachings are a Divine Message from our God (Allah) and I want to make sure that my people understand it.

My teachings constitute God's own (Supreme) Wisdom, and my people (the so-called Negroes) would do well to accept it today. This is the only way to their Salvation, and Allah will soon prove it to those who do not want to believe.

ISLAM IS THE SUPREME WISDOM

I could not do a better job of ex-

plaining the true meaning of "Supreme Wisdom" than to say that it is Islam, the religion of the Supreme Being (Allah), our God, who came to us in the Person of Master W. F. Muhammad. So what could be better for us (the so-called Negroes) than to accept it as *our* religion?

FOREVER FREE !

We are today made deaf, dumb and blind. Islam will give us a new life and growth. Our slavemasters have had us in bondage to them for four hundred years. Islam will make us FOREVER FREE! It will also put us on top of the world as rulers of our own.

POWER, LIGHT AND LIFE

There are some of my people who doubt that Islam has power. They know not that Islam CAN and WILL give them power because it is from Allah (God). And who possesses more power than the All-Powerful Allah?

In addition to power, Allah is also the source of all light and life. Islam, of which I here write, will thus also give my peple (the so-called Negroes) Light and Life.

OPPOSERS BY NATURE

Islam is your *own* religion and that of your righteous ancestors (members of the Holy Tribe of Shabazz, the world's Original People). But the devils (your open enemies) oppose it for you and tell you to stay in their false religion of Christianity.

Do you know, my people, why the white Christians want you to stay Christian and stay away from your own (Islam)? Not because they have such love for their religion. No; they do not want you to accept Allah as your God because they are *by nature* opposers of Him (Allah) and His religion (Islam). No good is in the essence that the devils are from, and you and I cannot expect an evil people to tell us anything that is true and good.

JESUS WAS NOT GOD OR SON OF GOD OR EQUAL OF HIM

An example of how the white Christians love to lie can be found in their teaching of Jesus.

Jesus had said in his suffering, "My God, my God, why hast Thou forsaken me?" (Matthew 27:46) This indicates that he did not consider himself to be God or a son of God or equal of Him. Yet the white Christians believe in and worship Jesus as God or "son of God" or an equal of Him.

There are many other Bible verses which prove that Jesus was only a man

and prophet of Allah (God). Here I give three: "Is there a God besides Me? I know not any." (Isaiah 44:81, 45:22) "I am God, there is none else." (Isaiah 46:9) "One God and none other." (Mark 12:32)

THE ROOT OF IGNORANCE

A vast majority of my people (the so-called Negroes) here in America are completely ignorant to the knowledge of self and Allah (our God) and His religion (Islam). The root of their ignorance is the Bible, which they believe in and read but understand not at all.

It is the Bible, for instance, that has taught my people to believe in a God other than Allah, though it is He (Allah) Alone who is worthy of worship.

THE DISBELIEVERS' REWARD

Allah (our God) says in the Holy Quran, "Do those who disbelieve think that they can take My servants to be friends besides Me? Surely we have prepared hell for the disbelievers. That is their reward because they disbelieve and held My messages and My messengers in mockery." (18:102-106)

It is clear that the disbelievers referred to in this verse are none other than the Christians, who make mockery of the Holy Quran and Muhammad and other messengers of Allah. (Matthew 23:29-37)

80

My people (the so-called Negroes) should pay special attention to the "Reward" Allah promises the disbelievers in the above verse, and think for themselves why they must not lose any time in shedding Christianity.

UNNECESSARY MIX-UP

If you ask the Christians, "Who made the heaven and the earth?," immediately they will say, "God." They will not say, "God-the-Father-and-Son and the Holy Ghost."

If you ask them, "Who will give life to the dead on the resurrection day?," they will reply, "God." They will not say, "Jesus."

If the Christians know the true answer to such questions, they should then avoid unnecessary confusion or mix-up in their teaching of God (Allah), especially when teaching my people (the so-called Negroes).

THE GOOD LIFE

My people, Allah (God) wants you to lead a Good Life, and not one of evil, misery and sin.

Stop believing and following the devils, who are enemies of Allah and also enemies to you. They cannot help you in this life and if you remain in their names and false religion you won't even see the Hereafter. Be not afraid of them; fear Allah, and Allah alone, for it is He who is your Maker and Protector. Accept Him (Allah) as your God (which He is)

and His religion (Islam) and He will put an end to your miseries and suffering overnight.

Stop eating the filthy hog, which kills your mental power, and stop drinking wine, whisky and beer. All these and tobacco and drugs are forbidden by Allah. You must also stop gambling and committing indecent acts. You must make yourself completely righteous (return to Islam) or, Allah has declared, you will be destroyed from the face of the earth.

"YOU CAN HAVE IT"

I know it will take time for the unbelievers of my people who are willing to accept Allah as their God and His religion (Islam) to correct some of their ways and habits. Allah will help them as they endeavor. But they must not waste a single moment in throwing back Christianity into the slavemasters' laps.

My people, just tell the white Christians, "You can have it for yourself. We want no part of your false, slavery religion as it is not from Allah."

Islam will get you immediate universal respect and justice, which the so-called Negroes haven't had or known for four hundred years.

EVEN OUR SPIRITUAL "LEADERS" ARE BLIND

My poor people (the so-called Negroes) are the victims of every known cruelty and evil treatment known to mankind. This makes them fear their oppressors (the devils) even more than they fear God. When in trouble, they are so confused that they seek refuge in the enemy's brothers that they may punish their brother for the wrongs done to them. Worse yet, they go to their preachers who further disgrace our race and kind by praying not to God (Allah) but to a dead man and prophet (Jesus) and an unknown God that they imagine is living in the skies.

This proves that even our (the so-called Negroes') spiritual "leaders" are blind and not in the right mental state.

These blind spiritual "leaders" sell themselves to be the friends of their people's enemies (the devils) and thus oppose their own salvation. May Allah help me to open my poor people's eyes before these (blind spiritual) "leaders" lead them to destruction with them.

MAY ALLAH HAVE MERCY ON MY PEOPLE!

Now that the devils know that their time (to rule the world of black mankind) is up and that Allah will soon free their slaves in America, they gladly put them (the so-called Negroes) on the air to preach, who shout out their ignorance to the public.

The poor slaves (my people) even think that they are being treated with honor, and in their ignorance, serve their masters' purpose and seek their friendship above Allah's (God's).

I pray, may Allah have mercy on my people in America!

WE LACK LOVE, UNITY AND SELF-RESPECT AMONG US

Never have there been a people on this planet (Earth) who were enslaved and yet they loved and worshipped their slavemasters, except the so-called Negroes who live under the very shadow of death in America and still they love their open enemies (the devils).

As if this wasn't bad enough, my people (the so-called Negroes) also lack love, unity and self-respect among themselves, which makes it even more difficult for us to gain recognition and respect from other nations of the world.

My people, give up your differences, and unite as one Nation (Islam). Love your black, brown, yellow and red brothers as thyself. Do good unto each other. Never think of shedding the blood of your own kind. You are a righteous people, so treat all human beings right. We must not do good only to self and do evil to others. (This does not mean that we should love the devils, but we must be righteous and act according to the law of justice.)

WHISPERINGS OF THE SLINKING DEVIL

I beg of you, my people, who are defenseless and completely at the mercy of every brute force in America, to FLY to Allah now and say, " I seek refuge in the Lord of men, the King of men, the God of men, from the evil of the whisperings of the slinking devil, who whispers into the hearts of men, from among the Jinn." (*THE HOLY QURAN, Chapter 114:1-6*)

And when you have sought refuge in Allah, you need not fear of the evil whisperings of the devil any more, nor should you be afraid of those of our people who have joined on to their enemies' side. The Muslim's righteousness will always sustain him against the world of Satan.

The whisperings of the slinking devil, of course, can cause much mischief and of grave consequences. But my people (the so-called Negroes) who are Muslims should hold fast to Allah and He will make them overcome all obstacles and mischief.

THE EVIL SEEDS

A characteristic of the devil is that he sows his evil seeds among such people who believe in him (not in Allah) and then shrinks back as though he has not done anything. Then he (the devil) delights in watching the growth of his evil seeds.

This is never better fulfilled than to-day among my people. The devil is well-pleased to see that his workings among the so-called Negroes of America have been successful. The Truth of him and his kind, however, will put a complete stop to the devil's mischiefs and he won't be able to fool us any longer.

Say: "As for me, my Lord has guided me to the right path, a right religion, the faith of Abraham, the upright one, and he was not of the Polytheists. My prayer and my sacrifice and life and my death are surely for Allah, the Lord of the Worlds—no associate has He, and this am I commanded, and I am the first of those who submit."

IT IS INFIDELIC TO BELIEVE IN OR TEACH OF TRINITY

I must warn you once again on this question—of "sonship to God" (the Trinity). It is not only foolish to believe in or teach of the Trinity but it is also purely infidelic and a sin. To claim that God has a son is to charge Him (Allah) with an act of adultery, and God is married to no woman. The teaching of it (Trinity) comes only from the devils who have always wanted and still want to prevent us—you and I— from believing in the One God (Allah).

UNITY OF OUR PEOPLE WILL GIVE US GREATER POWER THAN ATOMIC BOMBS

One of the chief purposes of Islam in America is to bring about unity of our people. Unity is the purpose of the Coming of Allah (God) and also the judgement of the world. There is nothing that my people (the so-called Negroes) need more badly than unity. When this is achieved, we would have a greater

83

weapon in our hands and possession than all the atomic bombs the West can manufacture.

Unite, my people, and regardless of your faiths and beliefs, form yourselves into one Nation of Brotherhood (the love and help of each other). You will see that unity will solve the greater part of your problems before you know it.

THE LATE NOBLE DREW ALI AND MARCUS GARVEY

I have always had a very high opinion of both the late Noble Drew Ali and Marcus Garvey and admired their courage in helping our people (the so-called Negroes) and appreciated their work. Both of these men were fine Muslims.

The followers of Noble Drew Ali and Marcus Garvey should now follow me and co-operate with us and in our work because we are only trying to finish up what those before us had started. In Islam alone we shall find the success we desire, so join on to the Nation now and give us a chance to help *all* of our people in America.

"BALAAM"

Some of the unbelievers of my people (the so-called Negroes) and their preachers (the black friends of the slave-masters) recently took a trip to Washington to pray to "Balaam" to have mercy on them and grant to them a place near to them. Did he ("Balaam") hear them and grant their plea?

The president of the United States and Congress, who make the laws and choose agents to enforce it on whom they please, have ignored my people (the so-called Negroes) for 400 years, and for at least one hundred years we have been reminding them, in vain, of what is written in their Constitution. Yet my people deem fit to go to "Balaam" and beg him for justice.

But you, my people, are not at fault for trying something that we know to be uselss. The fault lies with our so-called "leaders" who don't know any better.

My people, STOP BEGGING "Balaam" or his people to accept you as one of them or to give you justice. You will find the remedy of your ills in Islam and answer to your prayers in turning to your God (Allah). Give up Christianity and following blind "leaders" and save yourselves from destruction forever.

ADVICE TO THE SO-CALLED NEGRO NEWSPAPERS AND MAGAZINES

I would like to offer a few words of advice to the newspapers and magazines of my people (the so-called Negroes):

I believe they (the so-called Negro newspapers and journals) would make a wise step toward better respect if they would leave love potion and such filthy mess out of their publications. This love trash in our newspapers and magazines is ruining our younger generation to the extent that it is now a near-tragedy. The only way we can prevent our children from forming the habit of "going" for indecent pictures and stories is to completely rid our papers of such.

THE FINAL CALL

My last word to you (the so-called Negroes) in this book is that you pay heed to what I have stated in it, and do not doubt its truh.

Do no listen or pay attention to what the devils (your open enemies) say about these writings or me. Always remember, they once deceived the very people of Paradise (Genesis 3:13), killed their own brother (Genesis 4:8), and are indeed the shedders of blood (Rev. 16:6). The soil of America, soaked with the innocent blood of the so-called Negroes shed by their (the devils') wicked race, now crieth out to its Maker for her great burden, and the day has arrived for Allah to descend PLAGUE AFTER PLAGUE upon her until the wicked are completely destroyed.

The blood-shedders (devils), who never cease to do mischief and spill the innocent blood of my people, even plan to kill me—your brother who holds the only key to your Salvation—for teaching you the truth of self and Allah (God). But they don't know that Allah will soon give them (the devils) their own blood to drink like water and their arms and allies won't help them against Him.

The Final Call has been given out. It is now the time of DECISION. What is yours?

May Allah (your God and mine) enable you all to grasp His (Supreme) Wisdom and guide you to the Path of Eternal Success, Prosperity and Happiness (Islam).

Coming Soon!

Volume Three

of

The Supreme Wisdom

Don't Miss It!

1957

Are you in one of these pictures? If not —

They Bear

"If you do not believe in the truth of my teachings, take a look at the REFORMATION these have produced in my people." The followers of the honorable Elijah Muhammad bear witness to the fact that his Message HAS brought about "tremendous improvement" in them, both "individually and collectively."

No longer do they drink, gamble, smoke or "eat themselves to death." They have stopped "doing all foolish things, such as wearing half-naked clothes, dancing, swearing and cursing, and staying out late in the streets at night." They do not even

86

Moslem
Convention
Chicago, Illinois
26th February 1957

plan on being with us next February 26th.

Witness . . .

touch the forbidden foods now, especially "the dirty, filthy hog." Many of them have better jobs than before: a number of others have opened up their own businesses—restaurants, gas stations, grocery stores, laundry and dry-cleaning plants, shoe repair and barber shops.

Today there are only (about) thirty Muhammad's Temples of Islam around the country. As more and more people join on to the Nation, many new ones will be set up.

The so-called Negro press too—All praise is due to Allah! —has begun to give the teachings and work of Messenger

Mr. Elijah Muhammad was recently honored by the Weekly "Pittsburgh Courier" with the presentation of a "Courier Achievement Award." He is seen here accepting the Award from Mr. A. D. Gaither, circulation manager of the "Courier".

Elijah Muhammad the moral support it deserves.* The years to come may see the establishment of Muslims' own newspapers and magazines and even radio and TV stations here. "That would enable us to bring more of our deaf, dumb and blind (mentally-dead) people into the knowledge of their own."

"And when *all* the dead of our people have arisen," say the followers of Mr. Elijah Muhammad, "the whole world will bear witness with us to the greatness of our leader and teacher."

---

*A column entitled "MR. MUHAMMAD SPEAKS," written by Mr. Elijah Muhammad, is printed each week in the Weekly "Pittsburgh Courier." The column appearing weekly in the New York "Amsterdam News" is entitled "THE ISLAM WORLD." The Weekly Westchester (N. Y.) "Observer" prints the teachings of Messenger Muhammad in the form of a series entitled, "WHITE MAN'S HEAVEN IS BLACK MAN'S HELL.

Index

90

93

95

Thank you for purchasing this book. We trust the reading was rewarding and enlightening. We offer various titles and a comprehensive collection of Messenger Elijah Muhammad's works. These works include:

- **Standard Published Titles**
- **Unpublished & Diligently Transcribed Compilations**
- **Audio Cassettes**
- **Video Cassettes**
- **Audio CD's**
- **DVD's**
- **Rare Articles**
- **Year Books**
- **Annual Brochures**

You are welcomed to sample a listing of these items by simply requesting a FREE archive Catalog.

Our contact information is as follows:

Secretarius MEMPS Publications
111 E Dunlap Ave, Ste 1-217
Phoenix, Arizona 85020-7802
Phone & Fax 602 466-7347
Email: secmemps@gmail.com
Web: www.memps.com

Wholesale options are also available.

Made in the USA
Monee, IL
02 July 2020